Basics of ...

FLORIDA'S SMALL CLAIMS COURT

Basics of ...

FLORIDA'S
SMALL CLAIMS
COURT

An Explanation
For Everyday People

Albert L. Kelley, Esq.

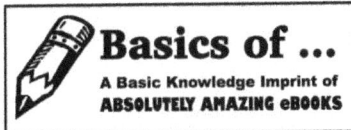

Basics of ...
A Basic Knowledge Imprint of
ABSOLUTELY AMAZING eBOOKS

Basics of ...

is an imprint of
ABSOLUTELY AMAZING eBOOKS

Published by Whiz Bang LLC, 926 Truman Avenue, Key West, Florida 33040, USA

For information contact:
Publisher@AbsolutelyAmazingEbooks.com

ISBN-13: 978-0692268407 (Basics of ...)
ISBN-10: 0692268405

Basics of ...

FLORIDA'S SMALL CLAIMS COURT

THANKS

This book was written with the help of my wonderful wife and editor, Angie Kelley, who has been correcting my mistakes for over two decades. Also thank you to my parents John and Martha Kelley and my aunt and uncle, Evelyn and Van Huyck who always encouraged my writing. This book is dedicated to them.

Table of Contents

INTRODUCTION

Small Claims Court. More people will experience small claims court than any other type of civil litigation. In 2012, out of the 463,978 cases filed in County Courts in Florida, 210,795 were small claims (the others were broken down by evictions [147,599], replevins [2,747], monetary civil litigation between $5,000 and $15,000 [99,847] and other [2,990]). With a population of 19.32 million people, that equals one small claims case for every 91 people, or in other words, one out of every 45 people will go to small claims court either as a plaintiff or a defendant (this ignores the people who go multiple times).

With so many people going to small claims court, it is important to know what it is, how it works and what the procedures are. Luckily, most people will never have to go to Court, but that also means those who do will often be facing a stressful, confusing system and process that they are unfamiliar with. The purpose of this book is to remove some of the confusion and in turn to alleviate some of the stress.

Let me begin by giving you my background. My name is Al Kelley and I am a lawyer, author, businessman, book publisher, film producer and college professor. I graduated with honors from Florida State University in 1989 and have been practicing law ever since. During that time, I have handled cases focusing on business law, corporations, entertainment law, contracts, copyrights, and trademarks. I have both prosecuted and defended criminal cases. I have also handled general civil litigation in the County, Circuit and Appellate Courts of Florida for both Plaintiff and Defendants. I was the Chairman of the Monroe County Career Service Council- a quasi-judicial agency. I am a member of the Florida Bar, and have been a member of the Trial Bar of the United States District Court for the Southern and Middle Districts of Florida. I have litigated countless cases in the small claims courts, for both Plaintiffs and Defendants. My clients have included individuals, small Mom-and-Pop businesses, national and international businesses. I also am the owner or co-owner of numerous companies. For several years I taught law courses at St. Leo University, and have written a weekly newspaper column on the law for three different publications, as well as authoring legal books, and teaching at numerous seminars.

Small Claims Court is also known as the People's Court. Not the People's Court TV Show, although the television show is essentially a small claim court (I will discuss Television Courts in the next section). But the real reason we refer to Small Claims Court as The People's Court is because it is designed to let the layperson appear before a judge and have their grievance heard without the strict procedural rules of the civil court system, without the delays of discovery, and without having to go through the expense of hiring a lawyer. That does not mean that you cannot hire a lawyer to handle your small claims case, and sometimes there are specific reasons for doing so, but we will get into that later.

This is not an exhaustive treatise on how to litigate

cases.   In law school students take an entire course on the Rules of Civil Procedure, another course on the rules of Evidence, another course on trial practice, and an entire year on research skills.   I cannot condense the details of those courses into one manual.   What this book will do is lay out the basics of Small Claims Courts.   While I will discuss the Rules of Small Claims, Evidence, Procedure and Research to some extent, this book cannot and does not replace legal advice and legal counsel.

Now for the mandatory disclaimer. The information being provided in this book is not designed to be specific legal advice. It is offered for information purposes only. It is not oriented towards any specific issue and through it, I am not representing any person or entity. The principles presented are based on Florida law (I am not licensed to practice in any other state and do not profess to be an expert on the laws of other states). If you have a specific legal issue that you need advice on, consult with an attorney of your choice.

I hope you find this book informative and entertaining, but mostly, I hope you find it useful.

TV COURTS

The People's Court, Texas Justice, Judge Hatchett, Judge Joe Brown, Judge Mathis, Judge Judy - these have been some of the mainstays in the lineup of reality television courtrooms. While many people try to ignore such frivolities as these, there is a benefit to watching these shows. What you find in TV courtroom is an instruction manual on how to present a claim or defense in small claims court. While other channels show real lawyers trying real cases, the trials they show are generally lengthy, complicated, and often boring events. While the hosts try to educate the viewer as to the interesting facts being presented, they offer little in the way of basic courtroom instruction. The reality television courtrooms on the other hand, provide short, simple matters where the basic rules are applied routinely and sometimes wrongly.

Now let me start with the most important point. What you are watching on a reality court show is not a trial. At best it is an arbitration and at worst a scripted fiction where all the parties are actors. The judges are not real judges, although some of them have been. Others are merely lawyers acting as a judge (Even Jerry Springer has gotten into the act with "Judge Jerry"). The judges are not holding a trial. They are not following any rules of court, or proper procedure. While TV Judges ask a lot of questions and try to guide the parties in developing their cases, this is not allowed in real courts. In a real court, the judge's hands

1

are often tied when people are representing themselves. In Florida, we have a specific rule that states: "In an effort to further the proceedings and in the interest of securing substantial justice, the court shall assist any party not represented by an attorney on: (1) courtroom decorum; (2) order of presentation of material evidence; and (3) handling private information. The court may not instruct any party not represented by an attorney on accepted rules of law. The court shall not act as an advocate for a party." So, while the Judges can advise the parties about how to act in Court, what sequence to present evidence and what confidential information they may not disclose about the other party, they must allow the parties to present their case as best they can without assistance. If the parties fail to prove essential elements of their case, the judge cannot coach them on what the elements are or what defenses are available. The judge must rule based on what the parties present. If they do not prove all the elements of their case, the judge must rule against them.

All of the reality courtrooms on television handle what are known as small claims cases (I will discuss this in the next section). Even the longest running court show, Divorce Court, which started as a scripted recreation of divorce hearings is now basically a small claims arbitration of debts between couples. In most shows that use real litigants, the parties have already filed a small claims case and agree to drop the lawsuit in exchange for binding arbitration on the reality court. Most of the time, the judges on these shows, while trying to be entertaining, also try to explain the rules of law that they use when determining their cases. They often explain not only the particular state law that governs a particular case, but general legal principles and evidentiary rules that will help the parties prevail on their case in other jurisdictions. Often they use general legal principles as the specific law is different from state-to-state. This is where the television courtrooms can be a benefit when you are preparing for Court.

The cases that appear on these shows are typical of the cases that usually appear in Small Claims Court, although the proceedings on TV are much less formal than you would find in a real courtroom. Also, the mistakes made by the people appearing on these shows are typical of the mistakes that occur in many small claims cases. By watching the shows and studying the proceedings that occur, a person may strengthen their ability to proceed and prevail, and may avoid the pitfalls that have taken down so many other cases.

Watching these shows, you will notice that the most frequent mistake made by the parties is the lack of proper documentation. This is the same in many small claims cases. If you are in business, you are expected to keep records, such as invoices, receipts, work orders, etc. If these are required to prove your case, have them available at the hearing. Do not bring copies. Copies can be faked; the Court wants originals. If you use a receipt book, it helps to keep the carbon copies in the book so the court can see the sequence before and after. Do not bring a check book register to prove a check was written; a check register proves nothing. Bring the cancelled check. Also, do not tell the judge that you forgot a document or that you did not think it was important. As a party to the lawsuit, you will not know what may become important at trial. Issues arise that are unexpected.   You will need to be prepared. It makes sense to have more than you will need, rather than not enough. If a document is even tangentially connected to the case, bring it.

Another mistake is asking for things that cannot be granted. One of the most common errors here is asking for lost time from work to appear in court, or asking for pain and suffering in a breach of contract case (pain and suffering damages are rarely awardable and only in specific types of cases-not breach of contract, and not in small claims). Study your available remedies before filing your case to ensure the Court can legally award what you are asking for. Another major mistake is not being able to prove your damages. If a plaintiff comes to Court and cannot document their actual damages, the Court cannot create damages for them. Unlike the Reality TV Courts where the judges often estimate damages or "split the baby", a real judge cannot award speculative damages or possible damages. Damages must be provable. I will discuss this later.

Courtroom television shows often display best the wrong way to do things. This is especially true in the parties' level of respect for the courtroom process. Routinely, parties on the courtroom television shows interrupt each other and talk over the judge. Often the Judges admonish them for such behavior. In a real case, a party should only interrupt the other party to object based on specific legal grounds. Simply shouting "He's lying!" is not a specific legal objection and will not endear the judge to your position. The judge realizes that you do not agree on what happened or you would not be in court. Let your opponent have their say and then the judge will give you your chance. It should be noted that the Court can proceed without a party's presence, so if a party refuses to stop interrupting, the judge can have them removed from the courtroom and still proceed with the case.

One of the greatest mistakes' television courts make compared to the real thing is in the area of hearsay evidence. Hearsay evidence is almost anything that is said by a third party outside the Courtroom (This is a gross oversimplification. Law school evidence classes spend weeks discussing what hearsay is and what the exceptions to it are, but we do not have that amount of space). The essential rule of thumb is this, if your proof involves the written or verbal statement of another person, the person who said it or wrote it must appear in Court. If they do not appear, their statement or the written document is not admissible, even if it has been notarized. This includes written repair estimates and police reports. These are not admissible unless the police officer or person making the estimate is present in Court to testify. And even then it may not be admissible. As an example, most police reports are written based upon what a person tells a police officer. So, while the report is hearsay for the officer's statement, the information is hearsay as to the person who spoke to the officer. Hearsay upon hearsay, you could say. There is a reason we don't allow hearsay in our courts: under our system of law, each party has the right to cross examine all witnesses. You cannot cross examine a piece of paper. If a party is attempting to show the Court a written estimate, the other side has the right to question the person making the estimate to determine if they have the necessary skill, knowledge, or ability to make the estimate. If there is a written statement, did the person writing it have all the pertinent facts in making it. The same is true for police reports (A major problem arises when a party tries to introduce a police report from an accident to prove the cost of repairs, since officers are not trained to give accurate repair costs). Notarization does not solve this problem. A notary does not swear that the details in a letter are true; at best they affirm that the person who signed the document claimed it was true.

In order to introduce a document written by a third party, or any statement made by a third party, you have the right to subpoena that person to appear in court and testify on your behalf. If they do not appear after being subpoenaed, the Court may continue the case to give them an additional chance to appear. If they still do not appear, they can be brought before the Court on contempt charges. I will discuss all of this in more detail later. The Reality TV Courts routinely allow documents in that have not been properly presented. Estimates are submitted without questioning and letters are introduced regardless of who wrote them.

Remember that TV Courts are there for entertainment. They are not trials-they are arbitrations, so the rules are more lenient. A better alternative to learn the process is to go to your local court and watch the small claims proceedings. The courtrooms are open to the public and the cases can be just as entertaining. One of my favorite moments in court occurred during a small claims case, and it wasn't even my case; I just happened to be in the court watching. A young man had sued three elderly men for money he had paid them for a casket he bought for when his mother passed away. He claimed that after he paid for the casket, the men used it to bury a relative. The young man had no paperwork to document any of his allegations. As the judge explained to the young man that he would have problems proving the case, two of the elderly men sat looking quite smug. The other elderly man asked to speak. He said, "Judge, I don't have much time left in this world and I can't go to meet my maker with a heavy heart." He paused and the said, "We did it, judge. We did everything that man said we did!" The other two men sat shocked and the judge suggested they all step outside to see if they could resolve the dispute. These are the types of things you only see in small claims court.

WHAT IS SMALL CLAIMS COURT?

Small Claims Court is not a special court; rather it is a special set of procedures and rules. This is true even if the County set up a special "Small Claims Court division". Small Claims matters are always County Court cases, just heard under Small Claims rules. Outwardly, it appears no different than County Court. Small Claims cases are generally heard in the same courtroom as County Court cases and they are generally heard by a County Court Judge (In Florida, there are four types of trial Judges- County Court Judges, Circuit Court Judges, Appellate Court Judges and Supreme Court Justices. There are also magistrates and administrative judges. While administrative judges handle matters for governmental agencies, occasionally the County Court will employ magistrates to hear Small Claim cases to assist with reducing the Judge's caseload. The magistrates, also sometimes referred to as Special Masters, do not rule on the case, but merely make a recommendation to the Judge who will issue a final ruling based on the recommendation). What is different are the rules and procedures that are used.

Small Claims Court is specifically designed and designated for "at law" cases that seek money or property valued in an amount between $0.01 and $8,000. The phrase "at law" means that the Small Claims Court cannot hear issues in equity. The difference between cases at law and cases in equity is a confusing one. Cases at law mean cases that are based in written law; while equity cases are based on what is referred to as "the common law"- legal issues that arise from historical usage. It is easier to think about it this way; legal cases are decided based on what a person is obligated to do; equity cases are decided on what a person ought to do. Equity often requests remedies other than the payment of money. This includes injunctions, declaratory judgments, or specific performance of a contract. The small claims judge cannot order an eviction, grant a divorce, or do anything but order the payment of money.

That being said, there are some actions typically thought to be equitable, which the Courts have deemed appropriate for small claims by determining that they should be treated as "at law" cases. These include actions for unjust enrichment, quasi-contracts, or quantum meruit cases (Quantum meruit literally means "as much as he has earned"). These actions ask the court to award damages because someone has done something to benefit another person, even though there was no actual contract. So for example, if two neighbors discuss splitting the cost to build a fence between their properties and the first one of them then proceeds to build it, thinking they have agreed to split the costs, and the second does not object to the construction, the first neighbor can sue the second for contribution because the fence has benefited the second neighbor. In other words, the second neighbor has been enriched and it would not be fair to let him keep the benefit without paying for it.

Also, the most the court can award is $8,000 (plus court costs, attorney fees [if allowed] and interest). If the Plaintiff's claim is for $8,001 to $30,000, the proper procedure is to file under County Court rules, not Small Claims, although a party can waive any amount over $8,000 in order to keep within the small claims jurisdiction. Why would they do that? There are a number of reasons.

First is financial. Small claims cases are designed to be less expensive than a County Court case. In some cases the filing fee is reduced, and often the service of process fee is reduced. The cases usually have less activity, so if you hire an attorney, the time they must spend on the case is usually less than for a larger case.

Second is ease of service. While a County Court case must be served on the opposing party by the sheriff or a private process server, a small claims case can be served by certified mail (but only if the opposing party is located in Florida). This cuts the cost of service by more than half. If the Defendant accepts the Certified Mail, they have been served and must appear in Court. If they refuse service or simply do not receive the mail, the court will continue the case to allow the paperwork to be sent to a second address, or to have the Sheriff or private process server attempt service.

Third is the ability to proceed without an attorney. In County Court, by law, corporations must be represented by an attorney. In small claims cases, however, they may be represented by a corporate officer, or even just by an employee, if an officer, manager, member or partner gives them written authorization to represent the company (they must bring the written authorization with them to the Pre-Trial Conference). The only exception to this is when the Court deems the Plaintiff to be in the business of collecting on judgments. In that situation, the Court can Order the business to be represented by an attorney.

Fourth is time. While a County Court case can take well over a year to go to trial, in most cases a small claims case is over in just a few months. The rules are designed to get the case through the system in roughly 4 to 5 months. That being said, I have handled small claims cases that took over a year, but that is the rare exception, and generally only occurs when attorneys are involved.

Finally is ease of proceeding. While County Court strictly follows the Rules of Civil Procedure and the Rules of Evidence, the Rules of Small Claims are less stringent. The Rules of Small Claims specifically incorporate some of the Rules of Civil Procedure (mainly those involving time procedures, amendment of pleadings, representation of minors, substitution of parties, subpoenas, and discovery in aid of execution). This also includes discovery, which includes depositions, interrogatories, request for admissions and request for production of documents. Under the small claims rules, a party is automatically allowed discovery only if the other party is represented by an attorney. Otherwise a special request for discovery must be made. Regardless of the involvement of attorneys, to have all the Rules of Civil Procedure apply, a special request must be made to the Court at the Pre-Trial Conference. This can be both a help and a hindrance. I will cover these issues in more depth later in this book.

The Rules of Small Claims and the Rules of Civil

Procedure are available online. The Florida Bar provides pdf copies as a free service at www.floridabar.org . Look for the "Rules" section.

THE LAW

To prepare for your case, it is advisable to first understand some basic legal principles. First is to know where to find the laws that you may sue under in small claims. There are numerous sources of law, any one of which may affect your case.

The premier source is the Constitution. Not only do we have a Constitution for the United States, each state also has a Constitution. These documents are the cornerstone of all our laws. Their purpose is to set out the basic legal theories for their citizens and legislatures to follow. Therefore, they cannot be changed by statutes or the legislature; only by a vote of the people. Generally, small claims cases are not based on Constitutional law. A copy of the Florida Constitution is available online through the Florida Senate's website at https://www.flsenate.gov/Laws/Constitution

Next, we have the statutes, both state and federal. These are the laws passed by the state and federal legislatures. These laws regulate the activities of the citizens of the states and their local governments. There are currently approximately 48 Titles in the Florida Statutes, covering nearly 1,000 chapters, and likely tens of thousands of laws. Many of these laws are inapplicable to small claims cases, such as Section XXV on Aviation, or Section XII on Municipalities. However, you could have a small claims case against a municipality. These are likely going to be a primary source of law for your small claims cases. The statutes are also available online at the Florida Senate's website at https://www.flsenate.gov/Laws/Statutes

Related to statutes are ordinances. These are the laws passed by lower government agencies such as the City and County Commissions. They only apply to the citizens who live in their districts. Generally, these are not applicable to small claims cases, unless the violation of an ordinance has caused a financial loss. Most city ordinances can be found online at https://www.municode.com/

The next section of laws is the administrative regulations, such as the Internal Revenue Code. Administrative regulations are governed by the various administrative agencies such as the Securities and Exchange Commission, the National Labor Relations Board, and the Department of Business and Professional Regulation. These regulations have the weight of statutes, but are enforced by the agencies rather than the Courts. Again, it is highly unlikely that an administrative law might be the basis of a small claims action. The Administrative Code is probably the second longest set of laws, next to caselaw which we will discuss next. The rules are highly complex and detailed. The Florida Administrative Code can be found online at https://www.flrules.org/

As for the Courts, they are our next source of law. Decisions of the appellate courts, what we refer to as "Case law", has the weight of statutes. When the Court publishes its decision on a case, that decision becomes the law for all similarly situated cases before that court and all lower courts (Decisions do not control higher courts. In other

words, the Supreme Court is not controlled by the decisions
of the Appellate Courts, and the Appellate Courts are not
controlled by the Circuit Courts.   One of the purposes of
the higher courts is to review the decisions of the lower
courts-their appellate jurisdiction). The act of following
prior decisions is the theory of "stare decisis" (literally, to
stand by the decision). Prior decisions set precedent for all
future courts to follow until the decision is reversed by a
higher court. The difficulty here is that there are hundreds
of years of case law to research (the oldest reported cases go
back to the 1880s) and it is often difficult to find the cases
that support your argument.   However, almost every case
you will bring in small claims will be similar to a case that
has been heard before, perhaps not in small claims, but in
County or Circuit Court, and case law is a great resource to
use to build your case. Because caselaw goes back so far and
so many cases have been reported, this will be the single
largest source of law in Florida. Unfortunately, there are no
easily available online sources for all caselaw for non-
lawyers.

Next, we have the common law. These are rules and
principles that derive their authority solely from custom
and usage. Florida law is based on the laws of England.
When the Florida Legislative Council first met in 1845, one
of the first things they did was to adopt the "common law"
as it existed in England on July 4, 1776.   These laws were
not written in statute books but came from Court decisions,
some of which are more than 800 years old.   On top of
that, the State also looked to Spanish laws from the years
under Spanish rule (There are Spanish laws that reach back
to 1597).   Today, the common law is still not found in the

statute books but is followed and can be enforced. As an example, a businessman who adopts a name for his store can prevent any other person from using the same name in the same locality, even if the name is not registered as a trademark. This "common law trademark" is fully enforceable in the court system. While common law can be the basis for a small claims case, it is not easily found. Usually you can locate it through case law.

So how do all of these sources of law affect you? Because the courts act under the theory of stare decisis, if you can find a prior case that has the same issues as your case, or if you can find a statute that addresses your situation, it will heavily influence the Judge's decision. Ideally, this research would be done before you file your case, so you know where you stand before you spend time and money. The question is, how do you find it?

In today's electronic world, legal research is easier than ever, although that does not mean easy. As mentioned before, the Florida Constitution and Statutes are readily available online. Aside from the senate versions already mentioned, the Florida Legislature has posted them online as well at www.leg.state.fl.us and you can find them through other sites as well. While there is a search feature on the legislature's website, unless you know specifically how to phrase your search terms, it may give you an excessive amount of laws to review. It may be easier to start with a review of the Titles in the Table of Contents and then when you find one that looks like it may affect your case, read the names of the chapters inside. Unfortunately, the terms used in the Table of Contents can be confusing. As an example, if your case is based on a promissory note, which you might think would be under Title XXXVIII for Banks and Banking, it actually comes up under Title XXXIX-Commercial Relations, and then look at Chapter 673-Uniform Commercial Code-Negotiable Instruments (a promissory note is what is called a negotiable instrument because it is a written promise to pay money, which can be transferred or sold to another person or entity). For a breach of contract, you may want to review Title XLI-Statute of Frauds, at Chapter 725-Unenforceable Contracts, and also Title VII-Limitations at Chapter 95-Limitations of Actions; Adverse Possession.

As an aside, Title VII-Limitations at Chapter 95-Limitations of Actions; Adverse Possession should be reviewed in EVERY case. This is the statute of limitations and will let you know how long you have to bring a suit. For example, a lawsuit based on a written contract must be brought within 5 years, but for a verbal contract, within 4 years. After those time periods, the lawsuit is improper and can be thrown out. Other cases that have a five-year statute of limitations include foreclosure cases and non-payment of minimum wage. Four-year statute of limitations applies also to (among other things):

- negligence actions
- an action based on the design
- planning, or construction of an improvement to real property
- an action to recover public money or property held by a public officer or employee
- an action for injury based on the design, manufacture, distribution, or sale of personal

property
- an action founded on a statutory liability
- an action for taking, detaining, or injuring personal property
- an action to recover specific personal property
- a legal or equitable action founded on fraud
- an action to rescind a contract
- an action for money paid to any governmental authority by mistake or inadvertence
- an action for a statutory penalty or forfeiture or an action for assault, battery, false arrest, malicious prosecution, malicious interference, false imprisonment, or any other intentional tort.

Florida also has a two-year statute of limitation for, among other things:
- an action for professional malpractice
- an action to recover wages or overtime
- an action for wrongful death
- and an action for libel or slander

Lastly, there is a one-year statute of limitations for:
- an action for specific performance of a contract
- an action to enforce an equitable lien arising from the furnishing of labor, services, or material for the improvement of real property
- an action to enforce rights under a Letter of Credit
- an action against any guaranty association
- an action to enforce any claim against a payment bond on which the principal is a contractor, subcontractor, or sub-subcontractor

- an action to enforce a claim of a deficiency related to a note secured by a mortgage against a residential property that is a one-family to four-family dwelling unit.

Many times it is difficult just to know what Title in the Florida Statutes to look at. Here your search engines (Google, Bing, etc.) are helpful. A simple search on Google or another search engine for "Florida contract law" will likely give you over 170,000,000 records, but if you specify "Florida Contract Statutes" by scrolling through the first few pages of results can provide a number of starting points for your research, including what statutes to review. Today, a carefully worded search online can provide tremendous research capabilities, however, make sure you back-up all your research. I do not mean back-up like make a copy. Here back-up refers to other sources. There are a lot a false websites. Just because one website says the law is "X", do not trust that. Look for other sources that confirm it.

The other difficulty is that there may be statutes which put specific requirements that can limit your recovery. As an example, Florida has a statute called the Statute of Frauds (Florida Statutes 725). This has nothing to do with fraud as most of us know it. The statute states that in certain circumstances a contract must be written to be valid. Generally, in Florida the contracts covered under the Statute of Frauds include any contract made in consideration of marriage; any lease for longer than a year; any guarantee or assurance made by a health care provider as to the results of any medical, surgical, or diagnostic procedure performed by any physician, osteopathic physician, chiropractic physician, podiatric physician, or dentist; for any contract that cannot be completed within one year; any contract for sale of land; and any contract where one person agrees to pay the debts of another person, living or dead. If any of these contracts are made by verbal agreement, they are not enforceable. The writing required by the Statute of Frauds does not require a formal written agreement, signed and notarized. It may be merely a memorandum or letter stating the terms. So long as it is signed by the party it is being used against and contains all of the necessary terms of the agreement, it may be sufficient.

A Statute of Frauds contract is generally voidable, not void. It is what we call an "affirmative defense". In other words, it must be specifically pled as a defense at the beginning of a lawsuit or it cannot later be raised. As an affirmative defense, it does not deny the debt or obligation; it just says the debt cannot be enforced.

In addition, if your case involves the sale of goods, the contract might be governed by the Uniform Commercial Code. Florida Statute 672.201 states "Except as otherwise provided in this section a contract for the sale of goods for the price of $500 or more is not enforceable by way of action or defense unless there is some writing sufficient to indicate that a contract for sale has been made between the parties and signed by the party against whom enforcement is sought or by his authorized agent or broker." This means that if you have a verbal agreement, it may not be valid. Now, that does not mean you cannot file a Statement of Claim. Because these are "Affirmative Defenses", if the Defendant does not bring it up, the Court will likely let you proceed.

As you can see, it is important to fully research your claim (or your defense). You should expect to spend several hours, just on the research.

Unfortunately, case law is much harder to research than the statutes if you are not a lawyer. Years ago, each County had a county law library, usually located at the County Courthouse where the case books were readily available. This was a major expense as new cases are decided every day and the books are updated on a regular basis and new casebooks are issued every year. In addition, the law libraries carried not just the books on Florida law, but also Federal law and Administrative law. These days, the books are usually no longer maintained by the Court and research is done almost exclusively online. For lawyers, there are case law search services such as Fastcase and Westlaw that allow us to find cases rapidly. These are usually pay services that charge a subscription fee for their use. For the layperson who does not have access to these services, research of caselaw is not as easy. Check with your local County Library to see if they provide a free online legal research center. If not, you can still search the caselaw but not as easily. The Florida Supreme Court and the District Courts of Appeal have posted their opinions online, and they are searchable. For example, if you go to the Florida Supreme Court's website (https://www.floridasupremecourt.org/), and click on Opinions, there is a button to search all opinions. This allows you to search all appellate courts or select any combination of the courts. So, for example, I selected just the Supreme Court and searched "statute of frauds". The site gave me 372 matches. However, unlike the search engines used by attorneys, each match is produced in a pdf format with no summary, meaning I would have to click on each result and read the case to determine if it had bearing on my case. Still, this is a great opportunity for the layperson to do more complete legal research.

The public search engines like Google or Bing can also be helpful here. Major cases can be found online, but lesser cases can be difficult. If you can get the name of a case, you can then go the Supreme Court's website and look up the specific case.

You want to search for cases that are similar to yours and have the same basic facts. Most cases are written in the same format: Facts, Issues, Rationale, and Holding. The "Facts" are just that: the facts of that particular case. By reviewing the beginning of most cases, you can tell rapidly if the case is at all similar to yours. Even if the facts are vastly different, the case could still be beneficial though. "Issues" are the questions that this particular Court is trying to answer. Even if the facts are similar to yours, the Court may only be answering a specific question that has no bearing on your case. Or if the facts have no similarity, the issue could still be the same. "Rationale" is the theory that the Court uses to reach their answer. Often the rationale will cite other cases and may give you an idea of other theories to resea4rch. "Holding" is the final decision of the Court. Be careful in reading the Holding. In some cases there will be a majority opinion which is the actual holding, but another appellate judge may disagree and issue a dissenting opinion. This is not the law, but an explanation why he thinks the other judges got it wrong.

Nothing is more embarrassing and will lose your case faster than citing a dissenting opinion as if it were the law.

The only thing that may be more problematic than citing a dissenting opinion is giving the judge a case that has been overruled. Once you find a case that you believe benefits your position, research that case as best you can to make sure it is still valid.

While I can't teach you how to do legal research in this book (Law schools spend an entire year teaching students how to do legal research, and the skills needed are developed only through years of practice), I will attempt to give a thumbnail sketch.

First, the books. When dealing with Florida law, if you do not have access to the internet, there are five sets of books to be intimately familiar with. First are the Florida Statutes (Annotated if possible- the FSA). The Florida Statutes Annotated is a series of books that lists the Florida statutes in numerical order (There are over 900 chapters in the Florida Statutes and each Chapter has numerous statutes). After each statute, the book then lists a basic history of the current version of the statute and provides a list of some of the caselaw that has interpreted the statute. The FSA is quite easy to use and comes with a very comprehensive set of index books. The statutes and annotations are updated annually in what is referred to as a "pocket part" which is a booklet that is inserted into the back cover of the book. After reviewing the statute, you should be sure to look in the pocket part to see if the law has been modified or deleted or if there are new cases interpreting it. The annotation is simply just a sentence or two about how the case ruled on that statute. While the annotation may be helpful in clarifying the law, you should never trust the annotation to be correct. Occasionally, the annotation will be mistaken in the interpretation. When doing research, you should always read the complete case to ensure that it says what the annotation indicates.

The second set of books are called "Southern Reporter". There are actually three series of Southern Reporters. The first covers two hundred volumes covering cases from 1887 to 1941; the second series covers cases from 1941-2008 and the third series covers cases after 2008. These books hold all of the reported cases from the Florida Supreme Court and the Florida Courts of Appeal. This is where most of Florida law comes from. The books are not easy to use unless you know what case you are looking for. The Southern Reporter starts with a listing of all cases that appear inside.   This helps if all you know is the case name. While the books may have a small topic references in them, there are other books, which I will discuss shortly, that are better for looking up topics. The Southern Reporters are best used once you know which case you want to read. Cases are cited by the name of the parties, book and page number where they are located along with the Court, and year they were decided. For example, a citation that reads: <u>Key West Polo Club Developers, Inc. v Tower Const. Co. of Panama City, Inc.</u>, 589 So.2d 917 (Fla. 3DCA 1991) tells us that the case involved the two parties Key West Polo Club Developers, Inc. and Tower Construction Company of Panama City, Inc.; that it was decided by the Third District Court of Appeals in 1991; and that a copy of the case can be found in volume 589 of the Southern Reporter, 2nd Series, at page 917. The portion of the citation that specifies the

Court can also simply say "Fla" which means the Florida Supreme Court, or it can say "Fla. App." Meaning one of the Appellate courts.

The cases inside the Southern Reporter tells you what the Courts have said about the law. The Court's rulings are binding on all lower Courts in the same district (the Circuit Courts must follow the rulings of the District Court of Appeals, which must follow the rulings of the Supreme Court). The binding nature does not go to similar courts; in other words, a ruling by the 3rd District Court of Appeals is not binding on the 2nd District Court of Appeals. This can make it confusing when two courts disagree. Which do you follow? Generally, the decisions of the Appellate Court that covers your region is the binding court. For example, let's say you are in Key West. Key West is in Monroe County which is included in the jurisdiction of the 3rd District Court of Appeals. If there is a dispute between the 3rd District Court of Appeal and the 2nd District Court of Appeal on a case in Monroe County, the Court should follow the ruling of the 3rd District Court of Appeals. The rulings of the other District Courts are only binding on the Monroe County courts if there is no conflicting 3rd DCA opinion.

Just because a case says what you want it to say, it may not be the law. The third set of books is the Shepard's Citations. Shepard's is little more than a book full of numbers and abbreviations, but those abbreviations are as informative as the cases themselves. Shepard's Citations tell what the current status of a case is. For this reason, Shepard's is one of the most important research tools available. Shepard's Citations lists every case that has been reported in Southern Reporters (all three series) and then lists every subsequent case that has mentioned that case, indicating which portion of the first case was discussed, whether it was in the main opinion or a dissenting opinion, whether the original case was followed or overruled, and which Courts have addressed the case. Without showing you the books, it is difficult to describe, but I will make an effort.

Referring to the case <u>Smetal Corp. v West Lake Inv. Co.,</u> 172 So. 58 (Fla. S.Ct. 1936). This is a very old case and has been mentioned at some point by every appellate court in Florida. Under Shepard's Citations, I looked this case up, first based on its book and page number. Occasionally, there will be two cases published on the same page, and Shepard's will indicate this as well. In my example case, it was the only case on that page. Shepard's then lists by book and page number all of the cases that cited <u>Smetal</u>, starting with those cases from the Supreme Court, then the Florida Appellate Courts in numerical order (1st, 2nd, 3rd, 4th, and 5th), and then the Federal Circuit Courts in numerical order. Next to some of the cases will be a letter. These letters tell how the following court referenced the cited case. The letters are as follows: a (affirmed), cc (connected case), D (dismissed), m (modified), r (reversed), s (same case), S (superseded), v (vacated), c (criticized), d (distinguished), e (explained), f (followed), h (harmonized), j (dissenting opinion), L (limited), o (overruled), p (parallel), and q (questioned). These letters are crucial as a case that has been reversed or overruled may no longer be good law. Also, a case cited in a dissenting opinion may conflict with the controlling decision. In the <u>Smetal</u> case, 8 court decisions had distinguished the case (meaning they explained why the Smetal case was different from the case they were deciding), two had followed it, and one had mentioned it in a dissenting opinion. Also next to the listed cases may be a comment such as "note 1". This refers to the "Headnote". At the beginning of each case published in the Southern Reporter, there is a group of small numbered paragraphs, summarizing the major points of the case. These are the headnotes. Each numbered paragraph starts with a topic and is followed by a "key number", a code created by the West Publishing Company. Key numbers are assigned to each topic and subtopic, to group cases together that cover the same points. While key numbers make research easier, if all you have are the headnote numbers, you can still research the topics through Shepard's. Often, you will only be interested in one particular point of the case. Shepard's lets you see which cases referred specifically to that headnote, so you don't have to look up other cases that are irrelevant to your issue. The Smetal case had over 24 headnotes. After looking up each of these cases, you can then "Shepardize" them to see if there are other cases you should read. Every case that is looked up should be reviewed in Shepard's Citations, if for no other reason than to ensure that it has not been overruled.

Not only does West Publishing Company publish the Southern Reporter series of cases, but also a series of books called West's Digest. The Digest is a collection of the headnotes listed according to key number. In other words, if you find a case that refers to the necessity of obtaining personal service on a party to a lawsuit, it will give a key number of "48" under the topic of "Process". This key number refers to the subtopic of "Nature and Necessity in

General". To find more cases that address this same issue, you would refer to West's Digest, look up the section on "Process" and then turn to section 48. Here would be a listing of headnotes from other cases that refer to the same point. Each headnote states the citation of the case it comes from, allowing the reader to locate other cases that may benefit their position.

To keep the Digests updated, there is a small pouch in the back cover of each issue. Here is inserted a booklet called a "pocket-part" which contains new headnotes issued since the last edition of the book was released. It is helpful to review the pocket-part after reviewing the digest itself to get the more up-to-date cases and to see if there are cases that seem to reverse prior holdings.

Of course, as I mentioned before, you cannot rely on the headnotes alone. Occasionally, a headnote itself will be incorrect. It is crucial that the actual case be fully read to ensure that the headnote is correct. After the case is reviewed, you must again "Shepardize" it (as described earlier) to ensure that the case has not been overturned, questioned, or reversed.

The last major book series to be familiar with is Florida Jurisprudence Second Series (referred to as Fla. Jur. 2d). This is a great book for summarizing general legal points. Fla. Jur. 2d is divided into various legal issues, and then each issue is subdivided into various points and sub-issues. Rather than simply list cases or headnotes, Fla. Jur. 2d is written in narrative style so that it is reader friendly. Those interested in learning the state of the law can simply read sections of Fla. Jur. 2d as if they were reading any textbook. As a research tool, Fla. Jur. 2d is a great asset. Throughout each narrative paragraph, Fla. Jur. 2d has numerous footnotes, citing to the cases that they relied upon for their information. However, as with the headnotes, it is important not to simply take Fla. Jur. 2d at face value, but to actually read the cases. They may not actually state exactly what Fla. Jur. 2d says they do. And like with the Digests, Fla. Jur. 2d is updated routinely with pocket parts.

It should be noted that neither the Digests nor Fla. Jur. 2d are actual statements of the law but should be used as reference material to find the law.

A final series that I want to mention are the Florida Law Weekly series. This is not actually a book set, but a series of booklets which contain those cases that were published by West Publishing Company during the previous week by the Supreme Court and all District Courts of Appeal. Because they are printed on a weekly basis, it is difficult to research through Fla. Law Weekly, but it is important that these cases be reviewed because at any time, a new case may overturn an older one. The last thing anyone wants to do is to give the judge a case that has been overturned.

If you live near a major city in Florida, you can locate these books at one of the law schools (there are currently 12 ABA accredited law schools in Florida: Ave Maria School of Law (Naples); Barry University School of Law (Orlando); Florida A&M University College of Law (Orlando); Florida Coastal School of Law (Jacksonville); Florida International University College of Law (Miami); Florida State University College of Law (Tallahassee); Nova Southeastern University (Ft Lauderdale); Stetson University College of Law (Gulfport); St. Thomas University School of Law (Miami Gardens); Thomas M. Cooley Law School, Tampa Bay

Campus (Riverview); University of Florida Levin College of Law (Gainesville); and University of Miami School of Law (Coral Gables). If a law school is not available, check with your local community college to see if they carry these books.

As mentioned before, online resources exist if the books are not available, but for non-lawyers, the search capability is not optimum. Some of the websites available are Findlaw.com, law.justia.com, Google Scholar (scholar.google.com), and the Public Library of Law (plol.org). Many layers have websites to discuss the law. There are other sources as well. I started by writing a weekly newspaper column on the law. I since write five lawbooks under the Basics Of . . . series. I have even created a YouTube channel titled "Basics Of The Law" with a series of videos based on my book series.

These legal sources will assist with doing legal research, however, it may take time to develop the skills to do it quickly. Most online sites will let you search by the name of one of the parties, lawyers, or judges, or by searching dates or keywords. Online research through these sites is often not as fast as research with books due to the search engine limitations. The difficulty is defining the issue you want to research. If your search is too broad, you will get back thousands (or millions) of responses; if too narrow, you may not get the response you need. For example, on Google Scholar, I searched small claims. I received back 2,560 responses. When I put the search into quotation marks ("small claims"), I received 322 responses. When I removed the "s" and searched "small claim", I received just 15 responses. Even with the best keyword search, be prepared to spend a great deal of time refining your search and reading many cases that will have nothing to do with your situation.

If you can research the statutes and case law, you will have a much stronger case to present.

STARTING A SMALL CLAIMS CASE

While most lawsuits begin with the filing of a Complaint, a small claims case begins with the filing of a Statement of Claim. While there is no specific format this must follow, for many people the easiest way to start is by filling out a small claims form you can obtain from your clerk of court. The form is only one page long and is fairly easy to complete. While they cannot give legal advice, the Clerk of the Court can greatly assist you with completing the forms and filing the case. The Clerk's Office handles countless small claims cases and know the ins and outs of the court process. These workers, who are often overlooked in the Court process, may be the most important people you will deal with outside of the Judge. Treat them with respect and they can be extremely helpful; treat them with disrespect and you will be doing nothing but giving yourself much more work.

The person or entity filing the Statement of Claim is called the Plaintiff and the person or entity being sued is the Defendant. This seems obvious but is the source of a number of errors which can lead to the case being dismissed. The Statement of Claim must be brought by the person who has been damaged or is owed the money. If a friend of the Plaintiff files the lawsuit on behalf of the

Plaintiff, it will be dismissed, unless the friend is an attorney. Florida does not allow a non-lawyer third party to file a lawsuit on behalf of another person. This would be deemed the unauthorized practice of law. While normally the Court will merely dismiss the action, if the person filing the Complaint has a history of doing this or if the local unlicensed practice of law committee (the UPL Committee) feels the person will be a repeat offender, the person can be required to sign a cease and desist affidavit, acknowledging they will not file any other Claims in the future, or they can be prosecuted before the Supreme Court, leading to a civil injunction and in extreme cases, criminal contempt of court.

The rules require that you include the name and address of the Plaintiff and Defendant. For the Plaintiff, this is usually not an issue. Just make sure that the proper party is listed; is the plaintiff an individual or their business? Also make sure to include the address. This is crucial. The Plaintiff's address is necessary so the Defendant knows where to send their response; the Defendant's address is necessary so they can be served.

The more problematic area is the Defendant. Plaintiffs need to be sure they are suing the right people. Often I see cases where the Plaintiff has named an individual when they should name a business, or even worse, when they try to sue an employee of the business. Employees have a limited immunity if they are doing their job. They can only be sued if their actions are outside of their employment responsibilities or if their actions are of a criminal nature. If the case is against a business (whether corporation or LLC), the Defendant is the business, not the officers, managers, or registered agents. The Plaintiff cannot sue the directors, officers, or managers unless they have done something outside of their corporate position, or if they have signed a contract as a guarantor. Like with employees, they have a qualified immunity if they are acting under their title as an officer, director, or manager.   As to the Registered Agent, this person may have no connection to the business operations at all.   A Registered Agent is simply a person appointed by the business to be served with lawsuits; not to be named in lawsuits.

Who and where you serve a lawsuit is another question the Plaintiff must know.   For an individual, they should be served at their place or residence, however, you may have them served at work or any other place they can be located. If choosing to serve by Certified Mail, it must be where they receive their mail at.   If the Defendant is a corporation or limited liability company, the process is different.   The address for the Defendant corporation will be the corporate mailing address or in the case of a limited liability company, the address of the registered agent.   These addresses are not necessarily the same as the business location.   To make sure you have the right person and address, check with the Florida Department of State at www.sunbiz.org. [Once at www.sunbiz.org, click on "Search our records" and then click "inquire by name" and type in the company name.   Now, there is a chance that the business name and the company name are not the same.   If this is the case, you will want to first search the business name by clicking "Inquire by fictitious name" and typing in the business name.   This will tell you who actually owns the business, and if an individual, their address.   If owned by a corporation or limited liability company, you can then search the corporation records on sunbiz.org to get its information and learn who the officers, managers and registered agents are].

Service on corporations and limited liability companies are not the same. If you are serving the case by Certified Mail, use the mailing address listed on Sunbiz.org. However, for service by the Sheriff or private process server, you need to know the proper procedure. To serve a company, you first attempt to serve the officers, President or Vice President first, then of not successful, on the Secretary or Treasurer. If you cannot serve them, then you try to serve a director. As an alternative, you may serve the company's registered agent. As a last stand only, you serve an employee at the business. For a limited liability company, you first serve the registered agent. If they are not available, you next serve the Manager or if run by a Member, then on the Member (to determine if the LLC is run by a Member or Manager, you can again go to Sunbiz.org and search for the LLC name. At the bottom of the page or that LLC will be a link to their Articles of Organization. Each LLC is supposed to specify in their Articles if they are managed by a member or a manager). If a Member or Manager is not available, after at least one attempt has been made to serve them at the business location, you can serve any employee in charge of the business during reasonable business hours. As a last case scenario, if none of the above are available, you serve the LLC by serving the Secretary of State.

Next, need to state basically what the case is about. If you are using the form provided y the clerk, there is usually a space just to check the reason. If you are not using the clerk's form, just put in a simple sentence stating: "This is an action based on . . ." Then explain why you are suing. Did you sell something to someone and they did not pay you? Did you provide a service to someone and they did not pay you? Did someone breach a contract with you? Did you receive a   bad check? Did you loan someone money and they not pay you back? Did the Defendant start an account with you and then not pay? Did a tenant not pay you rent? Did someone damage your property?   If using the clerk's firm, just mark the category that fits closest to your category.   If none of them fit, there is usually a catch-all for "Other".   Most of the categories on the form are self-explanatory, however, mistakes do get made.

Next, write a short statement about what happened. If using the clerk's form, there is a small space for this, although you may need to attach an additional piece of paper if the facts are longer.   But usually, just a brief explanation will suffice.   If the lawsuit is based on a contract, a promissory note, an invoice, a lease, or any other written document, you MUST attach a copy of the document to the Statement of Claim.   If you fail to attach the document, the case can be dismissed.

Finally, put down the amount you are owed, up to $8,000 (do not include your filing fees. These will be added automatically by the judge if you win).   These are called damages.   Again, this seems pretty simple, but many people make mistakes here.   There are three types of damages: compensatory, nominal, and punitive.

Compensatory damages are the amount necessary to compensate the plaintiff for his loss. They equal the amount actually lost by the plaintiff or the amount needed to put the Plaintiff in the position he would have been in if there had been no issue or breach. These are the damages you see most often in small claims court.

Sometimes the court feels that the plaintiff should recover something, but there is no actual monetary loss, or the loss is extremely minimal. The court can award what are called nominal damages. These are generally small awards, often only $1 and are basically awarded just to give the plaintiff a moral victory. Because small claims court is dealing with smaller amounts of money, the Court will usually not award nominal damages.

Punitive damages are awarded to the innocent party to punish a wrongdoer. Punitive damages are awarded in excess of the actual compensatory damages. As a general rule, punitive damages are not allowed in contract actions. The reason for this is that in a capitalist society there are often business reasons to breach a contract (perhaps a cheaper supplier is found, or a contract will take too long to complete and another person can complete it faster). Because we live in a business society, we do not want to punish people for trying to improve their business. Punitive damages are an equitable remedy and therefore not allowed in small claims cases.

Damages also can be divided into direct and consequential damages. Direct damages are those that spring directly from the breach itself. A consequential damage is one that is related to the breach, but not because of the breach alone. In other words, it is not necessarily a foreseeable damage. Let's go with an example. I buy a new car and the brakes fail the next day. That is a breach of contract, because the car was not in the condition it was warranted for. I can recover damages for the repair of the brakes. These are direct damages, as they are directly related to the breach of contract. If because of my brake failure, I get into an accident and there are other damages to the car, I might be able to get recovery for this as well, as these damages are foreseeable and arise directly from the breach. What if because of the brake failure and subsequent accident, the stress gives me a heart attack? This is not reasonably foreseeable and leads to what is called a consequential damage. It also is generally not compensable in a contract action. (This does not mean it wouldn't be covered under a product liability case or a personal injury action. Just not a breach of contract action.). Consequential damages are generally not allowed in small claims court, for the same reason as punitive damages- they are deemed an equitable remedy.

In Small Claims cases, the Court cannot award punitive damages. They are limited to compensatory damages up to $8,000. They also cannot award pain and suffering, even though many Plaintiffs feel they should be entitled to it (If you want to make a claim for punitive damages or pain and suffering, file in County or Circuit Court).

Another mistake that occasionally arises is when a party seeks liquidated damages. While allowable, they can be questioned. Liquidated damages may only be sought when a contract contains a clause that guarantees a specific amount to be paid as a liquidated damage in the event of a breach. Liquidated damages are allowed when actual damages cannot be readily discerned. The amount of the liquidated damage must not be excessive. If it is too large, the court may look at it as a penalty, and it will not be allowed.

Generally, a party has a duty to mitigate damages if possible. This means that you have to take action to minimize the amount that the other party must pay. Let's say I have a two-year employment contract and am wrongfully fired from my job after just one year. I have a cause of action against my former employer for the salary I would have earned for the second year. However, I cannot just sit back and sue without doing anything. I must try to obtain new employment in the same field at approximately the same salary. If I succeed in getting a new job, the award of damages will be reduced by the income of the new job. I would not, however, be required to accept a job that is substantially different or that pays substantially less than my previous job. If a person fails to attempt to mitigate damages, the Court can refuse to award any damages. This issue rarely arises in Small Claims, usually when a Landlord is suing for unpaid back rent. The tenant has a proper defense if the Landlord made no attempt to re-rent the property.

The amount you are seeking must be a provable amount. Don't just write in an estimate of what you think you are owed. Don't just write in $8,000 because that is the maximum you can put down, unless your actual damages are more than $8,000.00. Put down what is actually owed. Many people make the mistake of adding other charges. For example, they will add in time they lose at work because they have to go to Court. This is not awardable. Sometimes people will add in legal fees because they met with a lawyer, when the case does not allow an award of attorney fees (I'll get into that issue later). What damages are allowed is what you are owed, and any expenses directly related to it, such as bank fees for a bounced check. You do not need to add the amount of the court filing fees as that will be added automatically if you are the prevailing party.

If you want a jury trial, the Plaintiff must request it in the Statement of Claim; otherwise the case will be heard only by the Judge. The Defendant can also demand a jury trial but only during the first five days after being served with the Statement of Claim or at the Pre-trial Conference. While jury trials are a right in Florida Small Claims cases, they are rare. Most small claims cases are heard only by the Judge (Jury trials are more difficult and take much longer than trials by the Judge. Also, if the parties do not know how to properly present their case, the jury may just get confused).

Once the form is completed, it must be signed and notarized. If the Plaintiff is a corporation, it should be signed by the President; if an LLC, it should be signed by the Manager. If you are completing the form at the Courthouse, the Clerk of Court can notarize it for you. Otherwise, you will need to get the form notarized before filing.

You will want to provide the Clerk with three copies of the Statement of Claim, along with all attached documents. The original will go into the Court file; one copy is given back to you with the case number written on it, and the third will be sent to the Defendant.

Once the Statement of Claim is filed and the filing fees have been paid, the Clerk of Court will give you a Notice to

Appear. This Notice is for your Pre-Trial Conference. Pay close attention to it, as the instructions on the form are crucial. If you have chosen to serve the Defendant by certified mail, the Clerk will send a copy of the Notice, along with a copy of the Statement of Claim to the Defendant. If you choose to serve them through the Sheriff or private process server, the clerk will give the Defendants copies back to you for delivery to the process server.

Once the Defendant has been served, they may file a Counterclaim against the Plaintiff for any claims they may have. If the Counterclaim is for $8,000.00 or less, the case will remain in Small Claims Court. If the Counter-claim is for an amount in excess of $8,000, the Court will remove the case to the County Court (or Circuit Court if the Counter-claim is over $30,000.00), and the standard Rules of Civil procedure will then apply. The Defendant (now called the Counterclaimant or the Defendant/CounterPlaintiff) will have to pay any additional filing fees required. The Counterclaim may be filed at any time up to and during the Pre-Trial Conference.

THE PRE-TRIAL CONFERENCE

If you filed your Statement of Claim in person, the Clerk will likely hand you the Notice to Appear for the Pre-Trial Conference. If you mailed it in, it will be mailed to you. The Pre-Trial Conference will be scheduled no later than 50 days from the date the Statement of Claim is filed. It is generally the first hearing in all Small Claims cases (Most Small Claims cases have no more than two hearings- the Pre-Trial Conference and the Trial). It is crucial that you attend the Pre-Trial Conference. If the Plaintiff fails to attend the Pre-Trial Conference, the Court will dismiss the case and if the Defendant fails to attend (after being properly served) the Court will enter a default against them (If you provide the Court with a valid and sufficient excuse why you missed the hearing, the Court MIGHT set aside the Dismissal or Default).

While this is not the trial date, you need to be as prepared as if it was. The Notice of Pre-Trial Conference generally has specific instructions on it. It will instruct you to be prepared to explain to the Judge the nature of the case and any settlement efforts you have made; to show the Court any documents you will be providing at trial; to name any witnesses you will use; to estimate how long the case will take and to stipulate to those facts that do not require proof. The reason for all of this is to give the Judge enough information to determine how the case should proceed. It also allows the judge to determine whether there is a claim sufficient to let the case proceed.   If the Court decides there is not a sufficient claim, they may issue a summary judgment denying the claim.   You do not need to have your witnesses present at the Pre-Trial Conference; the Court will not be taking any testimony.   And while the Judge will ask about the basics of the case, the Judge will likely be hearing many cases between the pre-trial and the trial dates, so while the Judge may remember some aspects of your case, he (or she) will not remember the details sufficiently to have established any predisposition to it.

While this is not the trial, you want to present yourself as if it were.   Arrive early.   If the Judge calls the case and you have not yet arrived, it is the same as not attending. The case can be dismissed or a default entered.   It is not wise to show up wearing work clothes (unless you work in dress clothes).   While you do not need to wear a suit, it is advantageous to wear clean trousers and a dress shirt; for women, a nice outfit- pants or below the knee dress and a dress blouse. Do not wear dirty clothes or torn outfits.   Do not wear shorts or mini-skirts, half-shirts, tank-tops, sandals, sunglasses, or hats.   Lawyers are taught in law school to show respect for the Court.   That is not just in how we address the Court, but also how we dress. While the phrase says, "Justice is blind", the judge is not.   Your appearance can make a difference.

Likewise, when you are talking to the Judge, maintain a respectful tone and refer to the Judge as "Your Honor" or "Sir" or Ma'am".   Do not use slang terms or say "Yeah" for "yes" or "nah" for "no".   Answer questions properly, not with head nods. Do not interrupt the Judge or the opposing party. And never address your comments to the opposing party during the hearing; address them to the Judge.

When the hearing starts, the first thing the Judge will do is review the file to determine if the Defendant has been served.   If the Defendant is in the Courtroom, it is usually conclusive evidence that they were served (but not always). If the Defendant is not in the Courtroom and there is no evidence in the Court file that the Defendant was actually served, the Judge will continue the case to allow more time for service.   If the file indicates that the Defendant could not be served by Certified Mail, the Judge will continue the case and allow you time to serve the Defendant personally by the Sheriff or a private process server (to do this, you will need to return to the Clerk's Office, get a new Pre-Trial Conference Notice and a copy of the Statement of Claim with all attachments.   Take or mail this packet to the Sheriff of the County where the Defendant resides or if a business, does business. The Sheriff will charge a fee to serve the papers [Some Sheriff's will require that you also provide them a copy of the Property Appraiser's webpage showing the location of the property they will be serving to]. Once service is made, the Sheriff will file a Return of Service with the Clerk of Court and mail a copy to you, if you gave them a preaddressed envelope.   As an alternative you can contact a private process server in the County where the Defendant is being served. Private process servers may have other requirements, so make sure you speak to the before mailing the paperwork).

If the Defendant has been served but does not show up

for the Pre-Trial Conference, you have won. The Court will enter a default judgment on your behalf. While that sounds like it would be the end of the case, if the Defendant shows up later and gives the Judge a reasonable excuse for their non-appearance, the Court can set aside the default judgment and the case gets reset for trial.

If the Defendant has been served and is in the Courtroom, the Judge will call both parties to the front of the Courtroom. At this time, the Defendant can file a Motion to Dismiss (We will discuss this in the next Chapter). If no Motion is filed, or if the Judge denies the Motion, he or she will generally ask each side to briefly state their case and list their documents and witnesses. The Defendant also has the right at this time to admit liability and request a repayment schedule, advising the Court how he desires to pay the amount. The Plaintiff may accept this payment schedule but is under no obligation to. If the Court allows the repayment, the judgment in the case may be held in abeyance while the payments are made. If the Defendant makes all the payments as promised, the case is dismissed; if not, the Court may enter judgment against the Defendant for the full amount, minus any payments already made.

If the Defendant does not admit liability, the Court will often send the parties to mediation. Many counties have put together a special mediation program for small claims cases. Generally, this is a free service and often helps the parties resolve their case without going to trial.

Mediation is not a trial and the mediator is not a judge. Rather he (or she) is a facilitator who tries to help the parties negotiate a settlement. It is an informal process with really only three rules. First, it is confidential. Essentially anything said during the course of mediation stays in the mediation (there are a couple of statutory exceptions, primarily dealing with admissions of criminal activity or child abuse). In other words, if the Defendant admits liability in the mediation, but the case does not settle, the Plaintiff cannot tell the Judge that the Defendant admitted liability during the mediation. Also, the mediator cannot be called as a witness to testify as to what happened during the mediation. The second rule is related to the first: if the mediator wants to meet privately with the Plaintiff or Defendant, anything said in that private meeting cannot be told to the other party without consent. In other words, if the Plaintiff tells the mediator, "I know I asked for $5,000, but I would settle for $1,000", the mediator cannot tell that to the Defendant unless the Plaintiff authorizes him to do so. The reason for these two rules is to encourage people to communicate. Communication can resolve more cases than the Court can. The third rule is that if the case is settled, the settlement is written down and signed immediately. The settlement can be structured any way the parties agree- it can include a lump sum payment, or a series of payments. It can include all, part or none of the amount requested. This settlement is then signed by the Judge and becomes a binding Court Order which can be enforced immediately. Although mediation is a consensual process, each party must attend the mediation unless they are represented by counsel and have given their lawyer full authority to settle the case without consulting with the party. The party can also have a nonlawyer representative appear for them at the mediation, but again the nonlawyer representative must have full authority to settle the case. This means they have the right to sign the mediated agreement without having to call anyone else.

If the case is resolved in mediation, it is over. The parties must live with their settlement agreement and the Court will close the file, subject only to enforcing the terms of the settlement agreement.

If the case is not resolved in mediation, the Court will give the parties a trial date. Pursuant to the Small Claims Rule, the trial date is to be within 60 days of the Pre-Trial Conference. The Court will put this date in an Order, which is generally given to the parties before they leave the Courtroom. This is the only Notice the parties will receive regarding the trial date, so it is important that the document is retained and the date calendared.

MOTION PRACTICE

When most people think of lawsuits, they think of trials. However, the best lawyers do not always win cases at trial; often cases are won during what is referred to as Motion Practice. A lot of things are handled by Motion. In fact, there are so many possible motions that can be filed, it would take too much room to discuss it in too much detail. Here I will just discuss the primary Motions that the Court hears during Small Claims cases: The Motion to Dismiss.

A Motion is a request that the Court make a decision about a contested issue. It may be instructional or limiting. It may be positive or negative. The person who files a Motion in referred to as "the Moving Party"; the opposing side is referred to as "the Nonmoving Party".

Whenever a lawsuit is filed, the Defendant should always consider whether there are grounds to file a Motion to Dismiss. There are a number of grounds to dismiss a case, but the following are the primary ones:

1. **Failure to properly draft the Statement of Claim.** The Rules of Procedure mandate the information that needs to be on the Statement of Claim. For example, the Rules require the parties address to be included on the Statement of Claim. Generally, if the Plaintiff uses the forms provided by the Clerk of the Court, they will be in compliance with the Rules, but not always. And if they create their own Statement of Claim, the chance that they

forgot something is much larger. If the required information is not included, the Statement of Claim may be dismissed.

2. **Improper venue**. Venue means where the case can be heard. The general rule is that a case needs to be filed where the Defendant resides (or if a business, where they have an office), where the cause of action occurred, or where the evidence or property is. Regarding the first portion, note that the rule is where the Defendant resides- not the Plaintiff. The cause of action can mean different things. If it is a contract case, the cause of action is where the contract was last signed or where the payments were supposed to be made. For back rent, it would be where the real property is located. For injuries caused by an accident, it is usually where the accident occurred. Usually, if the case is filed in the wrong venue, rather than dismiss the case the court will transfer it to the proper location, but the Defendant will have to pay a transfer fee.

3. **Improper Jurisdiction**. Jurisdiction means what type of cases a Court may hear. It also indicates when a court may hear a case. The court does not have jurisdiction unless the Defendant has been served. If a defendant is never served with a lawsuit, the Court does not have jurisdiction over them and cannot hear the case. Jurisdiction also means the ability of the Court to hear a case. This covers area and issue. As to area, the Court only have jurisdiction in its region. If the Plaintiff resides in Florida and has a dispute with someone from New York but files in the case in Nevada just to make it more difficult for the Defendant, the Court has no jurisdiction because Nevada has no involvement with the details of the dispute.

In addition, in contract cases, the contract may stipulate that lawsuits must be brought in certain locations. If the Plaintiff files their small claims case in a place other than that stated in the contract, the Court will not have jurisdiction and should dismiss the case. As to topic, the small claims court's jurisdiction is limited to monetary cases under $8,000.00. They do not have jurisdiction to hear cases for more than $8,000.00. They do not have jurisdiction to issue injunctions, evictions, or divorces. They don't have jurisdiction to hear appeals.

4. **Improper party**. As I stated in a prior chapter, it is important to know who you are suing. Years ago, I handled a case where the Plaintiff had a potential claim against a business. However, instead of suing the business, they named an employee/officer of the business. Because they named the wrong entity, the case was dismissed. The Plaintiff then refiled the case, but this time named the company's registered agent instead of the company. While a registered agent's job is to be served with lawsuits, they often do not have any involvement with the day-to-day operations of the business. Whenever a claim is against a business, the business itself should be the named party; not a shareholder, employee, officer, or agent. Make sure you sue the right person.

5. **Failure to state a cause of action**. If the Statement of Claim does not allege a wrong that the Court can address, it fails to state a cause of action. In addition, if the Statement of Claim is based on a contract or other written document, a copy of the contract or document MUST be attached. If it is not attached the Statement of Claim fails to state a cause of action. In addition, if the

allegations in the Statement of Claim conflict with the terms of the attached document, it fails to state a cause of action.

6. **Improper service of process**. This is related to improper jurisdiction. If the Defendant is not served properly, the Court does not have jurisdiction over them. If the Plaintiff serves the Statement of Claim on the Defendant in any way other than allowed by statute, the case can be dismissed. Florida law allows a Statement of Claim to be served on a Florida resident by Certified Mail. So, if a resident in Michigan is served by Certified Mail it is improper service. If you use a private process server or the sheriff, they must follow the proper service rules. Occasionally they do not. Years ago, I had a case where the process server served a lawsuit on the Defendant's yard maintenance worker. The case was thrown out for improper service. Other times Complaints have just been left on the porch or sidewalk. The rules are specific- the Statement of Claim must be handed to someone over the age of 15 who resides in the house, and the process server must tell them what the document is. Any violation is grounds to dismiss the case. However, the Defendant must be careful how they draft the Motion. The Motion to Dismiss for Improper Service should be filed under the Court's "limited jurisdiction" solely to address the issue of service of process. If the Motion does not specify "limited jurisdiction", the mere filing of the Motion could give the Court jurisdiction and waive the defense.

7. **Failure to complete a condition precedent**. This is basically an argument that something must be done before the Plaintiff is allowed to file the Statement of Claim. As an example, a contract may state that before any action

is brought the parties must submit the dispute to mediation. If the Plaintiff has not yet gone to mediation, the lawsuit will be premature and can be dismissed or at least put in abeyance until the condition precedent is completed.

It is especially important that the Plaintiff is careful drafting the Statement of Claim. Normally, if the Court dismisses the action, they will allow the Plaintiff the opportunity to amend the Statement of Claim to correct the mistake. This is referred to as a Dismissal Without Prejudice. However, if the errors are such that the Plaintiff should not be allowed to correct them, or if the Plaintiff has already voluntarily dismissed the case two times (the "two dismissal rule"), the Court can dismiss the case "With Prejudice" meaning it cannot be refiled.

Aside from the Motions to Dismiss, there are other Motions that can be filed. Either party can file a Motion for Discovery. If the opposing party does not comply with the discovery request, the other side can file a Motion to Compel (I will discuss that in the next section). Either party can also file a Motion to Continue if the Court schedule conflicts with prior scheduled events.

While Motions do not have to be filed in writing in Small Claims Court (you can simply bring the issue up at the hearing), it is recommended that you do submit them in writing so you do not forget the argument you need to make. If put in writing, the Motion (or other document) filed with the Court must also be given to the opposing side prior to arguing it at the hearing. If the written Motion is brought to the Pre-Trial Hearing, a copy should be handed to the opposing party before it is handed to the judge and before it is argued. If drafted sufficiently before the hearing a copy of the Motion may be sent to the opposing party. If the opposing side is represented by an attorney, the Motion must be mailed to their attorney. At the end of each Motion or other document, it is advised that the Moving Party add a Certificate of Service. This is simply a signed statement saying essentially "I certify that a copy hereof has been furnished to (here insert name or names and address or addresses of the nonmoving party of their attorney) by (hand delivery) (mail) (e-mail) on .....(date)......", followed by the Moving Party's signature. The addition of this statement is deemed rebuttable proof that the pleading was provided to the Nonmoving Party.

The Defendant can also file a Motion for leave of Court to file a Counterclaim against the Plaintiff or a Third-Party Complaint. This is a lawsuit against someone other than the Plaintiff who may be responsible for part of the Plaintiff's damages. This can only be filed with permission of the Court which is generally requested at the Pre-Trial Conference. If granted, it will generally delay the case as the Third Party must be served and have time to prepare.

DISCOVERY

Discovery is the process of gaining information from the opposing side to help build your case or expose weaknesses in the opposing party's case. While Florida has a broad and liberal discovery policy in civil court, the rules in Small Claims Court are a little different. Discovery can be legally complex, so the small claims rules are designed to protect individuals who are representing themselves, and to keep these small cases from getting unreasonably delayed.

Generally, discovery is not allowed in small claims cases without permission of the Court. The exception is when both sides are represented by attorneys. If both sides are represented by counsel the general discovery procedures from the Rules of Civil Procedure apply. If the parties are unrepresented and either side wants to use the discovery procedures, they must seek permission from the Court first. If only one side is represented and the other is not, the represented party must seek permission of the court before seeking discovery, unless the unrepresented party has already sought discovery from the represented party. The Court generally has the discretion to allow or deny discovery. However, if one side is given the right to discovery, it applies to the other side as well.

There are basically four types of discovery: Request For Production, Interrogatories, Request For Admissions and Depositions.

Request For Production: This is just what it sounds like: a request (or actually a demand) for the opposing side to provide copies of documents that are related to the case. Florida's discovery rules allow a party to request copies of documents "regarding any matter, not privileged, that is relevant to the subject matter of the pending action". That is a very broad definition. What is relevant is often up for interpretation and Plaintiffs and Defendants often disagree on this point. Even if the item requested will not be admissible in Court, if the item appears reasonably calculated to lead to admissible evidence, it is allowable. So, for example, a letter from a friend discussing the case may be discoverable even if it cannot be introduced at trial as hearsay. Because it identifies the friend and what they may know about the case it is discoverable as it may lead to admissible evidence.

The responding party does not have to produce privileged documents. There are several privileges in Florida. We all have heard of the attorney-client privilege. There is also a privilege between a husband and wife, a Psychotherapist-patient privilege, a Sexual assault counselor-victim privilege, a Domestic violence advocate-victim privilege, a clergy-parishioner privilege, and an accountant-client privilege.

Within 30 days of receiving the request for production, the opposing side must either produce the documents or file written objections as to why they are not producing them. These objections must state specifically why they are not producing the document. The requesting party can then file a motion with the Court for an order compelling the production of the document. If the objection is without merit, the party refusing production can be penalized as if they had not responded at all.

Interrogatories: Interrogatories are written questions that the opposing party is required to answer under oath. While the opposing party is supposed to respond to these, if they are represented by an attorney, usually the attorney will draft the answers and the opposing party will merely sign them. Regardless of who actually drafts the responses, they are deemed the party's own words and therefore may be quoted during the trial. Like with the Request For Production, if the opposing party objects to the Interrogatories, the requesting party can seek an Order compelling the response.

Request for Admissions: These are a series of statements that the opposing party must either admit or deny. Those items they admit do not need to be proven at the trial. If the opposing party fails to respond to a Request For Admission, the statements are deemed admitted.

Depositions: A deposition is a formal procedure whereby the requesting party and opposing party meet before a court reporter. The requesting party asks the opposing party a series of questions which must be answered. If the opposing party objects to a question, they usually still must answer it. The objection is made on the record and before the deposition can be used at trial, the judge reviews the objection and rules on the admissibility of the answer. In very few circumstances the opposing party can refuse to answer a question- usually when the question involves a specific privilege such as the attorney-client privilege. However, under this circumstance, the requesting party has the right to seek an immediate hearing to get an Order compelling the other side to answer the question. If the opposing party (for example, we will say the Defendant, though this applies to both parties) fails to appear for his deposition, the Plaintiff may apply for a Writ of Bodily Attachment. This is a Court order to the local Sheriff to take the Defendant into custody to be brought before the Judge to explain why he failed to appear for the deposition. The Judge may then require the Defendant to post a bond to ensure that the Defendant complies with future discovery requests. Some judges will not issue these writs, viewing it as the same as debtor's prison which has been abolished.

If the opposing party fails or refuses to respond to any discovery request without sufficient grounds, along with an Order Compelling a response, they can also be sanctioned, including having to pay money to the requesting party, paying the requesting party's legal fees for both the discovery and the subsequent hearing, having pleadings or evidence stricken or in a severe case, having a judgment entered against them.

Statements made during discovery can be introduced during the trial and in some cases will be deemed to satisfy part or all of the elements of the Plaintiff's cause of action such that the Plaintiff does not need to produce any additional information.

While the timelines for discovery are specifically set out in the Rules of Civil Procedure (responses to a Request To Produce, Request for Admissions and Interrogatories are due 30 days from the date of service of the discovery request or 45 days from the service of the Statement of Claim if the discovery is requested at the same time), the timelines for discovery in small claims cases may be set by the court, even if that shortens the timelines normally allowed.

Discovery is a particularly important part of many lawsuits and due to the complexities and importance of how it is requested and answered, it probably should not be undertaken without an attorney.

TRIAL
PREPARATION

Everyone handles trial preparation differently. Some things need to be done though in every case.

Every case starts with planning. Remember the old adage: If you fail to plan, you plan to fail. In every case it is important to know the rules and what you are required to prove to win your case. Every cause of action in Florida has specific elements that must be proven in order for the Plaintiff to prevail. You need to know what these elements are. Then make sure your questions establish every point you need to make to establish those elements. Details are important. This is not a situation where you should try to "wing it". If you do not prove all of the necessary elements, you will not win.

How do you find the elements? I discussed the issue of Research in my chapter on "The Law", but to quickly find the elements of a cause of action, you can do a simple internet search with the type of claim you have (breach of contract, money owed, etc.) and the word "elements". I usually recommend adding the State name, as different states may have different elements for certain causes of action. A number of web sites will come up that give a list of what must be proven. For example, a search on Google for "Florida" "Breach of contact" and "elements" produced over 7 million results, However, the first was an article published in The Florida Bar Journal that said "The traditional elements of a breach of contract damages claim are well known to every law student: 1) the existence of a valid contract; 2) a breach of that contract; and 3) damages caused by that breach. There is no requirement that the breach be material for the other party to recover damages." The second site was from the Florida Supreme Court that states: "An adequately pled breach of contract action requires three elements: (1) a valid contract; (2) a material breach; and (3) damages." The third site was from a law firm that even breaks down the elements you need to prove to show there was a valid contract.

This sounds easy enough; however, there are issues to each of these elements. Was there really a contract, or did someone just promise to do something? Was the breach material to the performance of the contract, or just a minor difference in interpretation? Were there actual damages, or just a lower expectation?

Once you know what you must prove, you need to plan how you are going to prove it.   How will you testify? Will you need to call witnesses?   Will you need to produce any documentation?

If you have any witnesses that you want to testify at the trial, you should subpoena them. This is done for a few reasons.   First, a subpoena will give the witness a document that reminds them when and where the trial is. Second, it gives the witness a court order they can show to their employer to get time off work.   Third, and probably most important, it forces the witness to appear at the trial. If a witness tells you they will appear at trial without a subpoena and they do not appear, the Court will require you to proceed without the witness.   If, however, you give the witness a subpoena, and they fail to appear at the trial, the Court can reschedule the trial and sanction the witness for failing to appear.

Witness subpoenas are issued by the Clerk of the Court. To get them, provide the name and address of the witness to the clerk.   They will prepare the subpoena (there may be a slight cost).   The subpoena can then be served on the witness by anyone over the age of 18 who is not a party to the lawsuit.   However, if the witness does not appear, the person serving the subpoena may have to come to court to explain what they did to ensure the witness was served properly.

You also need to prepare all of your physical evidence. Knowing what evidence you need is crucial.   Without the necessary evidence, you cannot prove your case.   With too much evidence, you make the case confused.   There are certain evidentiary rules that are common in small claims cases.

If your case is based on a promissory note, you MUST have the original note.   A copy of the note is insufficient. While copies of contracts are allowed, a promissory note is a specific type of document. Only the holder of the original document may sue for the money owed on a promissory note.   If you lose the note, you can seek to re-establish it, but not in the Small Claims court. The original must be provided to the Court as it must be taken out of circulation. Otherwise, the Defendant can be sued again if another person gets a hold of the note.

If the case is based on a written contract, the contract

needs to be signed by both parties. If only one side has signed it, it is not a written contract, just written evidence of a verbal contract. If you only have an unsigned copy, it is not admissible because you cannot prove that the opposing party had agreed to those specific terms.

If your case is based on repairs, estimates cannot be used by themselves. A repair estimate is hearsay (Hearsay is any statement, including a written estimate, made outside of court that is offered to prove the contents of the statement). Instead of using an estimate, you will need to subpoena the person who made the estimate to testify how much they believe the repair bill will be.

Similarly, police reports are not admissible. Almost all police reports are hearsay. A police report is based upon statements made to the police officer. Unless the officer actually sees the accident or theft or whatever the police report is about, he is merely reporting what other people have told him (I will discuss hearsay in more detail later when I discuss objections).

Photographs are allowed, so long as they have not been modified or altered. The photographs must reflect truthfully the appearance of what the picture is of. Generally, the person who took the picture should be present to testify that they took it and that it reflects the scene at the time they took it.

Letters and affidavits, even if notarized, are not admissible. Many people make the mistake of bringing a sworn letter or affidavit. Notarization does not make a letter valid; it just certifies the existence of the person who signed it. Notarization is necessary for a document to be recorded with the clerk of court, but it has no validity in trial.   If the person who signed the document is not there, they cannot be cross-examined and therefore that evidence cannot be allowed.

It also is a good strategy to write out what you are going to say and what questions you need to ask your witnesses and what you are going to say as testimony.   This will help prevent forgetfulness that can occur under the stress of the trial.   A good way to do this is to start by listing what you MUST prove (Was there a contract? Was it signed? What are the terms? What was or was not performed? Etc.). Then write in what must be said to prove those points.

You also want to prepare as much as you can to challenge your opponent's case.   This can be difficult if you do not know what their defenses are. It sometimes helps to have a friend play devil's advocate to try and find weaknesses in your case.   However, you do it, rehearsal can be beneficial.

Be willing to spend some time in preparation. Web searches will give you differing results, and there can be several ways to present evidence or ask questions.   Find the ones that are most effective. You only get one chance to present your case, so make it count.

TRIAL

Many people have watched the televised court shows such as The People's Court and assume this is what small claims court is like. While the shows can be educational, they are not reflective of a small claims hearing. The problem with most televised court rooms is that the Judge participates too much. In Florida, by law, the Judge is allowed to assist the parties only on (1) courtroom decorum; (2) order of presentation of material evidence; and (3) handling private information. The Court is specifically instructed not to assist the parties with the accepted rules of law or to act as an advocate for either party. The Judge must stay neutral and allow the parties to present the evidence as they see fit. On the television courtrooms, the Judge acts as if they were a lawyer in many cases. They advocate for one side or the other. (This is not an indictment of television courtrooms. Some of the shows do explain certain evidentiary procedures and rules of court, and also can be informative as to how to present a case).

The procedure for a small claims trial is the same as for any other trial, however, it is less formal, which means some steps may be combined or even eliminated.

The first thing the Judge will ask is whether all parties are present. Just as with the Pre-Trial Conference, if the Plaintiff fails to appear, the case will be dismissed, and if the Defendant fails to appear, the Court will enter a default against them.   The Court will then take evidence just from the Plaintiff to ensure that the Plaintiff is entitled to a judgment and to determine the amount of damages.   The Court will then enter judgment for the Plaintiff and against the Defendant.

The parties may ask to appear by telephone.   This request must be made in advance of the trial and it is up to the Court whether they will allow this.   The party must show good reason why they cannot appear in person.   Also, if they are going to appear by telephone, they will usually need to have a notary public with them when the trial begins to swear them in (If they have hired a lawyer, the lawyer can also request to appear by telephone. As the lawyer is not a witness, he will not need a notary).   While telephonic appearance is allowed, it is not recommended.   Telephonic appearance does not eliminate or even minimize the evidentiary rules, and it is difficult to introduce documents when you are not physically in the courtroom.

Each party is generally given a chance to make an opening statement, with the Plaintiff going first.   This is not evidence, but merely a statement to advise the court what the party believes the evidence is going to show.   This is important because it is your first chance to tell the judge your story.   While the judge has your file, they will not know the details behind it. The parties should be careful not to overpromise during the opening statement.   It is not wise to tell the Court that you will prove something during trial that you cannot prove, or to make a statement when the evidence shows the opposite.   The opening statements should be factual and not argumentative. They also should be fairly short.

After the opening statement, the Plaintiff must present their case. The Plaintiff always goes first because they are the party with the burden of proof. If they cannot prove their case, it is over. How the case is presented is up to the Plaintiff. They can testify themself, call witnesses and present evidence (While the rules of evidence still apply, they are enforced liberally which means the Court may not be as stringent about the manner the evidence is introduced as they would be in a County or Circuit Court case). The Plaintiff an even call the Defendant to testify, although this may backfire. Lawyers have a saying- "Never ask a question you don't already know the answer to." When you call the opposing party, you don't know what they are going to say.

Usually the Plaintiff will start by testifying themselves. This gives them a chance to ell the entire story from their perspective and use other witnesses and documents to support their version of the facts. When they are finished, the Defendant gets to ask them questions about what the Plaintiff just testified to. This is called cross-examination. Cross examination is limited to the issues the Plaintiff discussed. In other words, the Defendant cannot bring up new issues during the cross examination. They can only ask about the same points the Plaintiff did. If the Defendant wants to bring up new issues, they can call the Plaintiff during their case. However, because the rules in small claims court are more lenient, the Courts will often give more leeway on the scope of cross examination.

After the Plaintiff testifies, they will call any witnesses they have to support their position. If the Plaintiff calls a witness (the Plaintiff is also deemed a witness if they testify) it is called direct testimony. Just as with the Plaintiff's testimony, after the Plaintiff finishes questioning a witness, the Defendant is given the chance to cross-examine that witness.

If the Plaintiff wants to submit physical evidence, such as documents or photographs, it is done through the Plaintiff's testimony or through a witness. Every document or exhibit must be properly introduced; you do not just hand it to the judge and expect it to be accepted. The item must first be shown to a witness who must identify the item and testify as to its relevancy and validity. Each item must be shown to the opposing party so they can inspect it and make any objections. It is then given to the judge for introduction as evidence.

Once the Plaintiff has called all their witnesses and submitted their evidence, they announce they have rested their case. This means they have nothing more to present. After the Plaintiff rests their case, the Defendant gets to present their evidence and witnesses, in the same style as the Plaintiff, allowing the Plaintiff to cross examine all witnesses and the Defendant. All that being said, check with the Court as to the procedure the Court will adopt. In order to save time, the Court may have the parties present their cases at the same time so witnesses do not get called more than once.

During the testimony phase, parties can object to questions they believe are improper. Despite what you see on scripted television shows and movies, you do not just yell "Objection". An objection must have a reason and the reason must be stated. There are specific grounds to objections; you can't just say "I object because I don't like the question". Objections must be timely and specific. There are three types of objections: objections that go to questions, objections that go to the answers, and objections that go to the introduction of evidence. If an objection is made, the witness must not answer the question until the judge rules on the objection. If the judge agrees with the objection, it is "Sustained" and the witness must not answer; if the judge disagrees with the objection, it is "Overruled", and the witness must answer (witnesses cannot object-only parties or their lawyers).

Objections to questions mean that there is an issue with either the question that is being asked or the witness's ability to answer the question. Some of the primary Objections to questions include:

1. **The question is ambiguous, confusing, misleading, vague, or unintelligible**: this means that the question is not precise enough for the witness to properly answer. If ranted, the opposing party can restate the question in a way that is clearer.

2. **The Plaintiff/Defendant is being argumentative**: the party's question is making an argument rather than asking a question.

3. **Asked and answered**: This occurs when the opposing party has asked a question, it has been answered and then he asks it again, possibly in a different way (attorneys often do this in order to stress a point)

4. **The question assumes facts not in evidence**: Here the opposing party is adding facts to the question that have not been established yet. For example, a question could be raised about a contract, before there has been any

proof that a contract existed.

5. **The Plaintiff/Defendant is badgering the witness**. This occurs when the opposing party is trying to provoke the witness into responding, either by mocking them or by asking questions so fast that the witness cannot answer them. This usually occurs on cross examination.

6. **Best evidence rule**: This objection goes to testimony about documents. If a witness is asked what terms are in a contract, the best evidence of that would be the contract itself. If the objection is allowed, the opposing party must either introduce the document in question or cease their line of questioning. This objection also goes to the originality of a document. If the opposing party attempts to introduce a copy of a document, the best evidence rule states that the original should be introduced, not a copy.

7. **Beyond the scope of examination**: This is an objection used during cross examination when the opposing party tries to discuss issues that were not raised in direct examination.

8. **The question calls for a conclusion**: Here the party is asking the witness not to testify about the facts, but about their opinion of the facts. While expert witnesses are allowed to testify about opinions, fact witnesses must testify to what they have seen or heard.

9. **The question calls for speculation**: Here the question asks the witness to guess at the answer rather than to rely on known facts.

10. **The Plaintiff/Defendant has asked a compound question**. This occurs when there is more than one question being asked at the same time. For

example: Where did you go and what did you do?

11.**Hearsay**: Okay. I have mentioned hearsay several times throughout the book and now is the time to explain it. Hearsay is defined as any statement made outside of the court that is being introduced to prove the matter asserted. What does that mean? Well, law schools take weeks (or months) to teach this concept. Basically, any time a witness is testifying as to what someone else said or wrote, it is hearsay. As mentioned before, this includes police reports, because the report is merely saying what someone told the police officer, repair estimates, because the party is asking the Court to consider what a mechanic wrote. The same is true for letters and affidavits. Hearsay is not allowed because our judicial system requires that the Court allow the opposing side to cross examine witnesses. A statement or writing made outside of the courtroom cannot be cross examined. If the court merely accepted a police report, the opposing side would not be able to cross examine the person who described the thief to the police officer to see if she really could see the thief. If the court accepts the estimate, the opposing party could not ask the mechanic about his experience and where he derived the numbers from. It is an issue of fairness and an issue of reliability. Now, all that being said, there are twenty-four exceptions to the hearsay rule. Without going into all of them, some of the most common are: If the statement is not being admitted to prove the issue in the statement, it may be allowed. For example, if a witness testified that the sky was green, the court may allow the testimony not to prove the sky was green, but to prove the mental state of the person who said it. Or if the opposing side wants to introduce a business document, if they can show that it is a standard document that the business regularly makes and it was made during the ordinary course of business and not for the purposes of litigation, the Court may allow it. If the statement is an excited utterance or made spontaneously at the time of an event, it may be allowed as there is more reliability when things are stated immediately. If the statement was made in another court proceeding, it may be allowed. It may also be allowed if it is a statement made against one's own interest. Hearsay is one of the most common and most misunderstood and complicated of all the objections. Few lawyers know it in great detail, so don't worry if you make a mistake.

12. **The Plaintiff/Defendant has asked a leading question**: This only applies to direct testimony as leading questions are allowed on cross examination. A leading question is one where the answer is given to the witness. "You went to the restaurant, right?" is leading. "Where did you go?" is not.

13. **Privilege**: Here the witness is protected from answering based on a specific privilege. Florida recognizes the attorney/client privilege, the psychotherapist/patient privilege, the journalist privilege, the accountant/client privilege, the sexual assault counselor/victim privilege, the domestic abuse counsellor/victim privilege, and the husband/wife privilege. Any question about a conversation that occurs between privileged parties is not allowed.

14. **The question is irrelevant or immaterial**: This objection raises the issue that the question is not about the issues in the trial. Sometimes parties will try to bring in

outside issues just to make the opposing side look bad, even when those things have no bearing on the case.

Objections that go to the answer are made after a witness makes a statement. They basically are asking the court or the jury to disregard what the witness has stated. The standard objections that go to the answer are:

1. **Non-responsive**: Here the witness has answered a question, just not the one that was asked of them.
2. **Narrative**: Here the witness is merely telling a story without being asked any questions. Our Court system is based on witnesses being asked questions and giving answers. While the Court may allow narrative testimony, it is not appropriate.
3. **There is no question pending**. Here the witness starts talking without any questions being asked of them,

Objections that go to the introduction of evidence include:

1. **Lack of foundation**: Here the Plaintiff/Defendant hasn't given enough details to warrant admitting the item into evidence. As an example, to introduce a photograph, the photographer should testify that he took the picture and that the photograph appears the same as the scene he took the picture of. This allows the court to assume that the photograph has not been tampered with. If the witness cannot state the above, the photograph should not be introduced. The same with a signed document. The party should first prove the signature on the document before introducing it into evidence.

2. **Incomplete**. If a party wants to introduce one page of a five-page contract, the evidence is incomplete. This objection instructs them to introduce the entire document into evidence so the court can read all of it.

3. **Hearsay** (addressed above)

You need to be quick with the objection. If the question is answered, it is too late to object. Objections are made to keep information out, but also to preserve issues for appeal and to throw off the other party's rhythm.

After both sides have finished their case, they get to present their closing argument. The closing statement is a summary of what the evidence showed and an argument as to why the evidence supports that party's position. Once the closing arguments are concluded, the Court evaluates the evidence and makes a ruling. Most of the time, the Court rules from the bench; this means that the Court makes a ruling immediately. If there is any complexity to the case, the Court may take the issue "under advisement". This means that the Court wants to take more time to evaluate the issue or research points of law before issuing a ruling. The Court then mails the final judgment to the parties.

If the Court enters judgment for the Plaintiff, they will also order the Defendant to pay the Plaintiff's court costs, including the filing fee and the cost of service of process (this includes the sheriff's fee if the Plaintiff had the Sheriff serve the Statement of Claim on the Defendant).

If the prevailing party hired an attorney, they can ask for an award of attorney fees, but the request must be made within 30 days of the Court's judgment, regardless of whether it is a judgment for the Plaintiff or the Defendant (If the attorney fee request was made in the Statement of Claim, an additional Motion will not be necessary. The Court can add the attorney fee award in the Judgment). Although you may be able to ask for fees, whether they will be granted is another question. Rarely can a party receive attorney fees for a small claims case. Generally, in Florida, attorney fees are only awarded in contract cases where the contract specifically allows for attorney fees (the same applies to promissory notes) and in other cases where authorized by statute (such as security deposit cases). There are very few situations where the statutes authorize attorney fees. Before hiring an attorney, it is important to evaluate the value of the case, whether it is the type of case where attorney fees can be awarded, what the likely outcome will be and what the likely attorney fees would be. Many attorneys will give a free initial consultation and can assist with this evaluation. It is not uncommon for attorney fees to be as much or more than the judgment amount in small claims cases. It is also important to remember that in litigation, if attorney fees would be awardable to one side, they are also awardable to the other. This means that if you lose, you may have to pay the legal fees for the opposing party.

REHEARINGS, RELIEF, AND APPEALS

U nlike other Courts, in Small Claims, if a party files a Motion and is not satisfied with the ruling, they must wait until after trial to address it. The Small Claims Rules have no procedure to ask for a rehearing or reconsideration of a motion. In other courts, under the Rules of Civil Procedure, a party may ask for a rehearing on any Motion if they believe the Court ruled improperly. This is not allowed in the Rules of Small Claims. Instead the Rules of Small Claims only allow for a Motion for a New Trial. There is nothing in the Rules which addresses a rehearing. However, if after the trial a party files a Motion for Rehearing, the Court can deem it to be a Motion for New Trial. This only applies to the trial though. Because the Rules do not allow for a rehearing, the parties cannot seek a reconsideration of any Motions the Court rules on.

A New Trial is not a right. The party requesting the new trial must provide the court with specific grounds for the new trial. While the Rules of Small Claims Court do not specify what grounds are necessary for a new trial, looking to the Rules of Civil Procedure and the case law, grounds would include the Court misapplying the law, newly   discovered   evidence   or   the   facts   being misunderstood.

After the Court makes its ruling, the parties have 10 days to file a "Motion for a New Trial".   This is an important point.   The ten-day time period is a strict time limit.   After ten calendar days from the day the court makes its ruling (not business days), it loses the ability to order a new trial.   Also, during this ten-day period the Court's Order cannot be enforced.   The Court does not have to hold a hearing on the Motion for New Trial.   The Court can simply review the Motion and if the Motion does not state sufficient grounds, the Court may deny it summarily.   In the alternative, the Court may decide it wants to hold a hearing and let the parties argue why the New Trial should be granted.

In certain circumstances, the ten-day rule does not apply.   If there was a mistake, inadvertence or excusable neglect, or if there is newly discovered evidence that could not have been known in time to ask for a new trial, or if there was fraud, misrepresentation or misconduct by the opposing party, or if the judgment is void, or if the judgment has already been satisfied, released or vacated, then the party may ask the Court to relieve them from the final Judgment.   The party must ask for relief within a reasonable time but not more than a year after the judgment was entered (unless the judgment is void or has been satisfied).

If a party believes the Court has ruled improperly, they can also request an appeal.   Appeals of judgments of the Small Claims Court are heard by the Circuit Court.   To seek an appeal, the party must file a Notice of Appeal within

30 days of the Judgment being rendered. Like the ten-day limit for a request for a new trial, the 30-day limit for an appeal is jurisdictional, meaning the Circuit Court cannot hear the appeal if the Notice is filed even a day late. Appeals are complex proceedings. I do not have the room to explain appellate procedures in detail. The shorthand explanation is as follows:

Within 30 days of the rendition of the judgment, the party who wants to appeal (called the Appellant) files a Notice of Appeal (plus applicable fees) with the Clerk of Court. The Notice must be in the specific format as recited in the Rules.

Within 50 days of the date the Notice is filed with the Clerk, the Clerk must prepare a copy of the file, along with an index and provide a copy of the index to each party.

Within 70 days of the filing of the Notice, the Appellant must file their "Initial Brief". This is the written pleading that states why the small claim court's ruling should be reversed or modified.

Within 20 days of filing the Initial Brief, the opposing party (called the Appellee) must file an Answer Brief, prepared in the same manner as the Initial Brief.

Within 20 days of filing the Answer Brief, the Appellant may file a Reply Brief addressing the points raised by the Appellee in the Answer Brief.

The format of the Initial brief is set out in the Rules of Appellate Procedure (Either Times New Roman 14 point font or Courier 12 point font; double spaced with margins at least one inch; footnotes and quotes in single space, bound in book form, etc.). The Initial Brief and the Answer Brief may not be any longer than 50 pages. If a

Reply Brief is filed, it will be no longer than 15 pages. The Initial Brief must contain a table of contents, a table of citations, a statement of the facts, a summary of the argument (2-5 pages in length), argument on each issue under appeal, a conclusion (no more than one page). Because of the highly technical format of the appellate documents, it is not recommended that the party file the appeal without the benefit of legal counsel.

The Circuit Court may review the Initial Brief and determine if it has alleged grounds for reversal of the lower Court's ruling. If not, the Circuit Court may summarily affirm the lower Court ruling and the judgment stands. If the Circuit Court finds the Initial Brief states a cause for reversal, the Court may then review the Answer Brief to see if it shows a meritorious basis not to reverse the lower Court's ruling. If no meritorious basis is shown, the Circuit Court may summarily reverse the lower Court ruling, sending the Judgment back to the lower Court to be corrected.

If either party would like to present oral argument to the Circuit Court, it must be specifically requested when that party's last Brief is due (For the Appellant- with the Reply Brief; for the Appellee, with the Answer Brief). Each side is limited to 20 minutes of oral argument. After oral argument, the Circuit Court will generally take the issue under advisement and later issue a written ruling which is mailed to the parties.

POST JUDGMENT

So you went to Court and won your trial. For example sake, let's say you won the maximum $8,000. Now what do you do? The Court helped you get the judgment, but they are not remarkably effective in getting you paid. We do not have a debtor's prison, so the Court cannot put the opposing party in jail if they do not pay you. However, the Court can still help you collect the judgment.

First, ask the Court to include the optional enforcement paragraph pursuant to Rule 7.221 in the final judgment. This paragraph states: *"It is further ordered and adjudged that the defendant(s) shall complete Florida Small Claims Rules Form 7.343 (Fact Information Sheet) and return it to the plaintiff's attorney, or to the plaintiff if the plaintiff is not represented by an attorney, within 45 days from the date of this judgment, unless the final judgment is satisfied or a motion for new trial or notice of appeal is filed. The defendant should not file the completed form 7.343 with the court. Jurisdiction of this case is retained to enter further orders that are proper to compel the defendant(s) to complete form 7.343 and return it to the plaintiff's attorney, or the plaintiff if the plaintiff is not represented by an attorney."* The court can also require the Defendant, if he was unrepresented during trial, to attend a hearing at least 30 days after the rendition of the judgment for the purpose of testifying under oath as to their earnings, financial status, and available assets.

What this does is require the Defendant to turn over to the Plaintiff their financial status. They must disclose all of their assets and bank accounts. They must provide their employment status and other forms of income. They must supply their spouse's financial information. They have to disclose real estate, wherever located, vehicles, and loans they have made to others. If they refuse to comply, the court can hold them in contempt and increase the amount they must pay. In some places refusal to complete the form has been held a direct contempt that can subject the Defendant to jail time until they comply.

Once you have the Defendant's financial information, you can start trying to collect the judgment. You must know where their assets are before you can seize them. When the Court enters a judgment, the clerk will record it. The first thing a party should do when they receive a judgment is to get a certified copy of the recorded judgment from the clerk and re-record it. This sounds strange because it has already been recorded. However, by re-recording it, your judgment becomes a lien against any real property the opposing party owns. This means the judgment has to be paid off with interest if the person sells or refinances the property. There is an exception to this. Under the Florida Constitution, homestead properties are exempt from judgments. While a judgment will create a lien on commercial or investment property, it does not create a lien on the debtor's homestead.

Next, if the person is employed, the Plaintiff can seek a writ of continuing garnishment against the Defendant's wages. This does not apply if the defendant is self-employed or works as an independent contractor- then there are other more timely and difficult methods to collect. But if they are an employee, the Court can order their employer to withhold up to 25% of every paycheck the employee receives until the judgment is satisfied.   Like many other things in the law, there is an exception to this: If the Defendant has minor children and is the head-of-household, they are exempt from garnishment.

If the Defendant has a vehicle, such as a car, you can seize the vehicle to pay the judgment, unless the car is worth less than $1,000, is leased, or if the Defendant has not yet paid the car off.   Any purchase money lien owed on the car takes priority over a money judgment.   In other words, if you seize the Defendant's car, you may have to pay off their loan.

If the Defendant owns other property (stereo, computers, etc.) the sheriff can seize the items and sell them at auction.   The debtor is allowed to select up to $4,000 of personal property that is exempt from sale (along with a vehicle worth less than $1,000).   None of these exemptions apply to corporations; only individuals. The sheriff is authorized to seize as much as is necessary to satisfy the judgment at auction, but no more.   To get the Sheriff to seize items, you will need to obtain a Writ of Execution from the Court and pay the sheriff's fee which can be several hundred dollars. This fee is added to your judgment amount and comes off the top at the auction. You also must give the Sheriff a form called Instructions For Levy. This form describes the property the Sheriff is to seize and where it is located.

Before the Sheriff sells the items at auction, you need to make sure there are no liens on it.   To do this, first go to www.floridaucc.com. This website keeps a list of secured debts. Type in the debtor's name and if any security agreements have been recorded with them, they will come up. Review the forms (called a UCC-1) and ensure the assets the Sheriff has seized are not included on them. If so, you will need to contact the secured party as their lien is senior to the judgment lien. Next you will need to check www.sunbiz.org to ensure there are no prior judgment liens registered against the debtor. Because judgment liens take priority based on recording dates, if there are any judgment liens recorded, you must also notify those parties. Once the Sheriff's sale occurs, the Sheriff will take his fee out of the sale proceeds. Next, he will pay you $500 for your costs, regardless of what the actual costs were. Next, the Sheriff will pay any prior judgment liens ahead of yours. Finally, if there is any money left over, the Sheriff will pay that to you, up to the judgment amount. If he has funds left over after your judgment has been paid, it is returned to the debtor.

There are certain things you can seize that tend to get faster responses than others. Pets are deemed property, so seize the family pet and see how long it takes to get paid. Wedding rings are also strong incentives. If your judgment is against a business, you can seize telephone deposits and have the business phones shut off until you are paid.

You can also get a court order freezing the Defendant's bank account. This locks down the Defendant's money so they cannot access it until the Court can order the bank to turn the funds over to you. To do this you need the bank location, and account number.

While all this sounds easy, it is not. Collecting a judgment is far more difficult than getting one. Many people are what we refer to as judgment proof. Either they have no assets, or the ones they do have cannot be seized. For example, retirement income cannot be taken. Therefore, if your judgment is against a retiree, collection may not be possible. In addition, if the Defendant has other judgments against them, yours may be too far down the line to be collectable. Finally, if the Defendant files bankruptcy, your collection efforts are over (If you try to collect a debt after the debtor has filed for bankruptcy, you can be held in contempt of court by the bankruptcy court).

There are other tools that can be used to collect a judgment and luckily, Florida Statute 57.115 allows a Plaintiff to get an award of attorney fees for having to take action to collect on a judgment. This is not absolute; the court has discretion to grant it or not. However, because of the attorney fee statute, once you have your judgment, it likely makes sense to hire an attorney to collect it.

SHOULD YOU HIRE AN ATTORNEY?

Do you need an attorney for a small claims case? No. Small claims is designed for people to be able to represent themselves. In fact, this is the only type of case where a corporation or limited liability company does not need to be represented by an attorney. They can be represented by an officer or even an employee.

Should you have an attorney? It depends. The first consideration is whether it is cost effective? A Small Claims case is a monetary action. Unless your sole purpose in filing is to aggravate the opposing party (yes, that happens), your goal is to get paid. If the legal fees are going to take a large portion of your potential settlement it may not be worth the expense. On the other hand, an attorney can save you time and worry. If you are represented by an attorney, the attorney can attend the Pre-Trial Conference in your place (as mentioned above, if the Court sends parties to mediation at the Pre-Trial Conference, you will need to give the attorney full authority to resolve the case in your absence). The attorney will also handle all of the research and trial preparation for you.

There are several items to take into consideration when deciding if you should retain an attorney for a Small Claims case. First are the legal fees. Legal fees can be billed in many ways:

Hourly: The primary billing method is hourly. In an hourly billing system, the attorney keeps track of how many minutes he works on a case and bills the client based on how much time he spent. As an example, if the lawyer bills at $300 per hour and spends thirty minutes on a hearing, he will bill $150. The problem with this fee arrangement is that the legal fees will fairly quickly meet or exceed the amount the Plaintiff is seeking. If the attorney bills more per hour, it will add up faster. At $300 an hour, the attorney only has to expend 26.6 hours before his fee has exceeded the statutory minimum for small claims. At $400 per hour it will only take 20 hours. Now, most small claims cases do not take that much time, but 4-5 hours is not uncommon.

Flat Fee: In a flat fee system, the attorney charges a fixed amount regardless of how much work he has to do. With the flat fee, the attorney makes the same whether he can end the case in one day or if it takes six months. The upside is that the client knows exactly what their cost is. The downside to this fee system is that it gives the attorney incentive to finish working more quickly, which may not always be in the client's best interest.

Contingent Fee: In a contingent fee case, the attorney gets a portion of whatever recovery the client receives. If the client does not receive anything, they don't have to pay the attorney. Usually the percentage is around 30% (Florida law set out a sliding scale for contingent fees that runs between 30 and 40%). Therefore, if the client receives a judgment of $1,000, the lawyer will receive around $300 of it, leaving the client with $700. This fee benefits Plaintiffs who cannot pay the attorney's retainer; however, it puts the Plaintiff and his attorney at odds with each other. While the Plaintiff may be willing to settle a case for a fraction of what he asks for, the attorneys would be better off to try the case for the full amount. As such, the attorney's may advise their client not to settle but go to trial, not because it is better for the client, but because it is better for the attorney. In the alternative, if the case is weaker, the attorney may propose a small settlement rather than taking the case to trial which could give the Plaintiff a larger payday.

Pro Bono: This is a free case for the client. Every attorney in Florida is required to do a certain amount of pro bono work or pay into a pool for others to provide free legal services. If the attorney determines that you qualify, they may be willing to work at no cost.

As mentioned in the previous chapter, in certain limited cases, the attorney can seek to have the other side pay his fees if he is successful. In these cases, if you have already paid the attorney, the funds will reimburse you for the fees; if you have not paid the lawyer, he will keep the portion of the judgment applied to his fees. It should be noted that if the court awards you legal fees, but the opposing party does not pay, you are still responsible for the legal fees.

The next item to think about is whether you can attend the hearings that might arise. Some business people will hire an attorney because they do not want to close their business during the hearings and feel it is worth the money not to have to attend. Other people have previous commitments or will be out of town during the Pre-Trial

Conference. Others simply live too far away to make attending the Pre-Trial Conference cost effective.

Then consider whether you have the ability or desire to do the work necessary to handle the case alone. While many people have the ability, they do not have the desire; others have the desire, but not the ability. If you are not sure of the legal process and are not comfortable with doing the work yourself, it weighs in favor of hiring counsel.

Also consider whether you are the Plaintiff or Defendant. While the Plaintiff is in a positive situation, facing receiving money or not, the Defendant is in a negative position, facing either paying money or not. While the worst-case scenario for the Plaintiff in most cases is the status quo; the Defendant's worst-case scenario is having to pay up to eight thousand dollars plus costs (and maybe legal fees). There is thus more incentive on the part of the Defendant to "lawyer up".

Finally, if the circumstances change, you may decide to hire an attorney during the course of the case, even immediately before trial begins. An attorney does not have to be hired at the outset. If during the course of the proceedings you decide it would be beneficial to hire an attorney, they can still make an appearance, even if it is moments before trial.

Once you file the Statement of Claim the Defendant may file a Counterclaim against you. At this point, both sides are facing a worst-case scenario and you may decide representation is needed.

CLOSING

Hopefully this book has provided you with some information on handling a small claims case in Florida. As mentioned at the outset, the information being provided in this book is not designed to be specific legal advice. It is offered for information purposes only. If anything you have read here has created questions regarding your situation, contact an attorney in your area. If you are not familiar with any, contact your state Bar Association for a list of local attorneys.

ABOUT THE AUTHOR

ALBERT L. KELLEY, is an attorney, author, book publisher, film producer, traveler and adventurer located in Key West, Florida. His law practice concentrates primarily in the areas of business, corporations, contracts, copyright, trademark, and entertainment law, as well as foreclosure defense. He graduated cum laude from Florida State University College of Law in 1989. He served for years as an adjunct professor for St. Leo University in their Business Administration program, teaching courses in business, employment, and administrative law. For five years Al wrote a weekly business law newspaper column and has authored a book on business law. He has also been a featured panelist at Florida State University's College of Law's Annual Entertainment Art and Sports Law Symposium. Albert L. Kelley serves as legal counsel for the world's largest offshore powerboat race promoter as well as museums, art galleries, television stations, performers, and newspapers. On the business side, Albert is corporate counsel to over 150 corporations, and has filed over 60 trademark registrations and countless copyright applications. Albert has negotiated contracts with numerous national companies including Apple Computers, Harley Davidson, and Ralston Purina. Al has given numerous seminars on trademarks, copyrights, film licensing and financing, and foreclosure defenses. He is a licensed skydiver, hang-glider pilot, and scuba diver. This is his third law book (Basics of . . . Business Law; Basics of . . . Florida's Landlord -Tenant Law).

Albert L. Kelley, Esq.

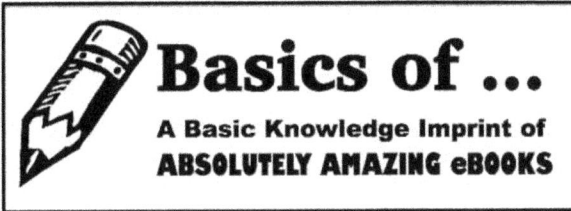

Basics of ...
A Basic Knowledge Imprint of
ABSOLUTELY AMAZING eBOOKS

AbsolutelyAmazingEbooks.com
Or AA-eBooks.com

www.ingramcontent.com/pod-product-compliance
Lightning Source LLC
Chambersburg PA
CBHW071515200326
41519CB00019B/5950